"Most books are good enough if they mirror back to the reader what is already known and provide a new version of interesting content, but this book is more than enough—it's brilliant! Monk Isaac Slater, OCSO, has done his *lectio*. We can read this book and learn how to do a restart of our practice."

— Sister Meg Funk, Benedictine nun, Beech Grove, Indiana, author of *Renouncing Violence*

"Navigating the complexity of human life with grace and a touch of humor, Isaac Slater moves us past the adrenaline rush of righteous indignation toward a practice of mercy. Drawing wisdom from both East and West, Slater overcomes the divide between me and you, us and them. Such an approach does not ignore sin, but rather refuses to let sin set the agenda. This is a wise and timely book in an age of division."

— William T. Cavanaugh, professor of Catholic studies, DePaul University

"Slater's *'Do Not Judge Anyone'* is a remarkable testament to just how great a gift the monastic vocation is to church and world alike. To a world and church often in thrall to phantastical images of self and others, images that distort the icon of God that lies hidden at the heart of every single one of us, Slater extends a spirituality characterized by that gentle, ruthless, peaceful, transparent, capacious, discerning, and eminently hopeful spirit that liberates us from our addiction to endless conflict. I will be using this lucid and accessible book in the classroom. Indeed, I will be returning to it again and again myself when I need to remember what it means to say: 'For freedom Christ set us free' (Gal 5:1)."

— Jordan Daniel Wood, assistant professor of theology, Belmont University

" '*Do Not Judge Anyone*' is a jewel of a book. It puts in full display Slater's many years of disciplined study and the keen insight that has resulted from it, leading the reader toward a wiser and more compassionate way of living in the world. Read with attention, curiosity, and humility, this meditation on non-judgment becomes a kind of *lectio divina*, or holy reading."

— Vanessa Zuisei Goddard, author of *Still Running: The Art of Meditation in Motion*

"A beautiful and honest reflection on what it might mean for us, personally and collectively, to refrain from judging others, and how the practice of non-judgment can help us create lives of healing love. Never have we needed this vision of inclusive love more than we do now."

— Douglas E. Christie, professor emeritus of theological studies, Loyola Marymount University, and author of *The Insurmountable Darkness of Love*

“Do Not Judge Anyone”

Desert Wisdom for a Polarized World

Isaac Slater, OCSO

LITURGICAL PRESS
Collegeville, Minnesota

litpress.org

Cover art: *Prayer of the Publican and the Pharisee*. Ivanka Demchuk. Used by permission.

Library of Congress Cataloging-in-Publication Data

Names: Slater, Isaac, author.
Title: "Do not judge anyone" : desert wisdom for a polarized world / Isaac Slater.
Description: Collegeville, Minnesota : Liturgical Press, [2025] | Includes bibliographical references. | Summary: "In "Do Not Judge Anyone" Isaac Slater, OCSO, reflects on the desert fathers' teachings and practice of not judging with a focus on contemporary life. Interweaving sources from East and West, ancient and modern, Slater finds points of contact between the first monks and figures like Dostoevsky, Simone Weil, and in the teaching and witness of Pope Francis"—Provided by publisher.
Identifiers: LCCN 2024044005 (print) | LCCN 2024044006 (ebook) | ISBN 9780814689738 (trade paperback) | ISBN 9780814689745 (epub) | ISBN 9798400801969 (PDF)
Subjects: LCSH: Judgment—Religious aspects—Catholic Church. | Desert Fathers. | Spiritual life—Catholic Church.
Classification: LCC BV4597.54 .S55 2025 (print) | LCC BV4597.54 (ebook) | DDC 241—dc23/eng/20250106
LC record available at https://lccn.loc.gov/2024044005
LC ebook record available at https://lccn.loc.gov/2024044006

Abba Poemen said to Abba Joseph, "Tell me how to become a monk." He said, "If you want to find rest here below, and hereafter, in all circumstances say, Who am I? and do not judge anyone."

—*The Sayings of the Desert Fathers*

~

When you include everything, that is the real self.

—Shunryu Suzuki, *Not Always So*

~

Until one has indeed become the brother of all, there will be no brotherhood.

—Dostoevsky, *The Brothers Karamazov*

Contents

Preface

> Every Religion that Preaches Vengeance for Sin is the Religion of the Enemy and Avenger and not the Forgiver of Sin and their God is Satan.
>
> —William Blake, To the Deists, from *Jerusalem*

On New Year's Eve 1998, exactly one year before returning to stay for life, I made a retreat at the Abbey of the Genesee. A monk gave a talk that included this story from the fourth-century Egyptian desert: monks came to their abba to report that a woman had been seen entering the cell of a certain brother. The abba stormed toward the scene shouting loudly about what he would do when he caught them. As he strode into the room followed by the breathless crowd of eager monks, he found the anxious brother, a laundry hamper, and not much else. He quickly went and sat on the basket and commanded the brothers to search the place top to bottom. When they failed to turn up the woman the abba chastised them roundly for accusing their brother and gave them all a stiff penance. When they'd slunk away he stood up from the hamper, turned to the brother and said, simply, "Be careful."

I was struck at once by the combination of humor, improvisation, and compassion in the abba's response, which struck me as fresh and radical, close to the spirit of Jesus, who had defended the adulterous woman and sent her accusers away humbled. Jesus' teaching and actions repeatedly stressed the need to "stop judging" and revealed the law that as we judge others we find ourselves judged in turn. "The measure you give will be the measure you get back" (Luke 6:38). Jesus embodied the way of not judging supremely on the cross when he gave himself away without expecting anything in return and asked his Father to forgive those who ridiculed and tortured him.

While the command to stop judging often seems muted in Christian tradition—if not effectively repudiated—the desert fathers and mothers give it a remarkable centrality. In fact, for them the essence of what it means to be a monk consists in not judging: "Abba Poemen said to Abba Joseph, 'Tell me how to become a monk.' He said, 'If you want to find rest here below, and hereafter, in all circumstances say, Who am I? and do not judge anyone.' "[1] There are many powerful sayings and stories in this line. This book is a kind of spiritual reflection on this material with a view to how it might call us back to the radicality of the gospel in a church and world so often enflamed by the spirit of the Accuser. Pope Francis who, in some respects, I will show, aligns with this strand of the desert monk tradition, describes the current moment this way:

> As the public arena has become increasingly dominated by the beleaguered self—anxious, controlling, quick to take offense, self-justifying—our society risks becoming ever more divided and fragmented. The Church is not immune to the contagion. How do we act in contexts of tribal division when our politics, our society, our media seem at times to be one long shouting match, in which opponents seek to "cancel" each other in a game of power? The growing verbal

[1] *The Sayings of the Desert Fathers: The Alphabetical Collection*, trans. Benedicta Ward, CS 59 (Collegeville, MN: Cistercian Publications, 1984), 102.

> violence reflects a fragility of selfhood, a loss of roots, in which security is found in discrediting others through narratives that let us feel righteous and give us reasons for silencing others. The absence of sincere dialogue in our public culture makes it ever harder to generate a shared horizon toward which we can all move together.[2]

It's become commonplace to speak of widespread intensifying "polarization" in contemporary life. Thinkers debate causes and remedies but clearly the new media play a critical role. A recent study showed the chemical response in the brain associated with the feeling of righteous indignation is akin to that produced by opioids. The surge of energy and empowerment, of rightness we feel when the host of our favorite podcast slams the opposition with some especially devastating jab, quickly becomes addictive.[3] Adrenalin starts pumping and a hit of chemicals we were meant to experience fleetingly in times of physical danger floods our system throughout the day as our phones ping with the latest. Corporate media boosts its ratings by catering to this addiction, stoking the flames of fear and grievance. In the context of deep-seated racial injustice, widening economic inequality and an emerging climate catastrophe on top of growing, often justified, distrust of big institutions the need for that "fix" of righteous indignation has become rampant, infecting even the quiet of some monastic cloisters. Suspicion and hostility toward big institutions and authorities extend to the storylines, the "meta-narratives" they profess and to some degree at least embody. At the same time we

[2] Francis, *Let Us Dream: The Path to a Better Future; Pope Francis in Conversation with Austin Ivereigh* (New York: Simon and Schuster, 2020), 76.

[3] James Kimmel Jr., *What the Science of Addiction Tells Us About Trump*, Politico, December 12, 2020, https://www.politico.com/news/magazine/2020/12/12/trump-grievance-addiction-444570.

are desperate for a story to believe in and those that provide the most intoxicating fix are sure to be popular. Fear feeds judgment. As Mark Edmundson writes in his recent essay on the Freudian superego today:

> The more affairs threaten to run out of control, the more it may help to have not only a firm position but a judgmental temperament. Judgment brings order. We go thumbs-up or thumbs-down and so appear to be the emperors of our own lives. Judgment is a great bulwark against chaos, or the perception of chaos. When we judge profusely and emphatically, we can feel that the world is our domain. Simplification and judgment: these are the ways we hold complexity at bay. Add to this the problem of a ravening cultural super-ego and you have a complex situation.[4]

While the "spreader-mechanism" of mass media may be new, the disease of punitive moralism arguably has roots in a Western Christianity that has too often clothed its own violence in distorted presentations of the gospel. In his book *Why Preach?*, Dominican Peter John Cameron argues that the number one problem with preaching in the church today is: moralism. As he writes, "To moralize is to enjoin a moral ideal on others without *explicitly* indicating how grace is the means for effecting it . . . without *explicitly* clarifying how the initiative of God enables the faithful to do what otherwise appears impossible . . . without *explicitly* revealing how the given course of action is integral to the realization of human happiness."[5]

[4] Mark Edmundson, *The Age of Guilt: The Super-Ego in the Online World* (New Haven, CT: Yale University Press, 2023), 86.

[5] Peter John Cameron, *Why Preach? Encountering Christ in God's Word* (San Francisco: Ignatius Press, 2009), 120; italics and ellipses original.

Moralism may be the "besetting sin" of the Western church, a deeply ingrained view that if the unfortunate would only *try harder* they would overcome their "disadvantages" and thrive. At the same time, just as an individual character grows strongest in the area where it is most often challenged, the church in the West holds a remedy to its own besetting sin in the doctrine of the gratuity of grace. From Paul to Augustine through Bernard to Luther and beyond a consistent if often drowned-out voice proclaims: "For by grace you have been saved through faith, and this is not your own doing; it is the gift of God" (Eph 2:8). God reveals himself in Christ crucified, hoping by this most gratuitous act of love to awaken in us a response in kind. Only within the horizon of unconditional mercy opened to us on the cross can we understand the desert fathers' teachings on the path of not judging.

But what is meant by "judging"? We are all judgmental, and judgmental thoughts flow through us constantly. We're not meant to wish them away or pretend they don't exist. We're not meant, surely, to stifle and suppress our outrage at injustice, to "forgive" in the sense of pretending to not feel grief and anger. Further, we make "judgments" all the time, evaluating situations and behavior continually. By "not judging" Jesus surely can't mean we give up thinking and making decisions. What then did Jesus mean by his command to stop judging? The kind of "judgment" we must renounce, I would argue, is characterized by condemnation, exclusion used as a way to boost our own esteem. Increasingly attached to this kind of judgment we rationalize our outrage like an addict justifying his need for another fix.

Like "judgment," "anger" too can hold different meanings. The momentary jolt of adrenalin meant to push us past fear to correct injustice is one thing and the smoldering resentment stoked by belligerent talk radio another. Jesus said clearly, "If you are angry with a brother or sister you will be liable to judgment" (Matt 5:22), while at the same time blasting the Pharisees and clearing out the temple in a state of what most of us today would call righteous anger. The desert fathers operated out of a (Stoic) tradition in which a "passion" was by definition a distorted and destructive energy. "Anger" as a passion was akin to wrath, a desire for vengeance, while zeal for justice, what we would call "healthy anger" was not considered anger at all. I would suggest that, while they require interpretation, the stories and sayings of the desert in which anger and judgment are essentially negative, can serve as a clarifying check on modern forms of righteous indignation.

Since entering the monastery I've been continually challenged, and have frequently failed, to walk the path of not judging. I've often been asked what sins a monk has to confess, living such a simple life, or what justifies a life of continual penance and conversion. But the atmosphere of quiet in the monastic cloister allows the inner world of the "thoughts" (*logismoi*) to grow audible and one realizes with dismay and alarm how deep within us lie the seeds of violence, rancor, and moralism. Living in close quarters with men from different backgrounds involves a daily challenge to check one's conditioned biases and relate to others at the level of faith and shared humanity. One needs constantly to see past half-conscious storylines and learn to work together with people of sometimes very different temperament and outlook.

It's often said that in the compressed environment of the cloister molehills quickly become mountains—and that's certainly true. But it's also often the case that everyday micro-frictions hold clues to subterranean energies that demand attention and healing. Dorotheos of Gaza likens the challenge of working with judgmental thoughts to a trade we learn only through practice and repeated failure. Speaking of the monk as such a workman he writes, "always he has to start by doing—and doing it wrong—making and unmaking, until, little by little, working patiently and persevering, he learns the trade while God looks on at his labor and his humility and works with him."[6]

The present book begins by mapping out some of the basic ideas that underlie my reading of the desert fathers on not judging, then turns to sayings from the Alphabetical Collection before exploring the more developed teachings on mercy and non-judgment in Dorotheos of Gaza and Isaac of Syria. A chapter on discernment as the right practice of which judgment is a distortion is followed by last reflections that include a number of texts from Pope Francis that challenge the church of today to walk the path of mercy and not judging.

Spiritual discernment is tied closely to the practice of a genuinely contemplative prayer. Just as I was finalizing the text of this book for publication, I happened to visit Gethsemani Abbey in Kentucky, where of course, Thomas Merton lived. I was able to revisit his grave, and hermitage, and to see, for the first time, the street corner in Louisville (then Fourth and Walnut) where he underwent a powerful spiritual experience that set his life on a new trajectory. I found myself quite moved by this, more even than I'd expected, as I pondered Merton's unique contribution, to the church, to monasticism, and to my own life. So I was feeling quite close to Merton when I happened across this passage in a book of his I hadn't looked at in maybe thirty years, a passage that puts its finger right on the insight at the heart of this book, namely, the connection between not judging

[6] Dorotheos of Gaza, *Discourses and Sayings*, trans. Eric P. Wheeler, CS 33 (Collegeville, MN: Cistercian Publications, 1977), 154.

as a feature of contemplative awareness and its expression in (moral) life. Commenting on a text by a Zen Buddhist author who describes spiritual consciousness as a mirror that simply reflects what arises without comment or judgment, Merton writes, "Here we can fruitfully reflect on the deep meaning of Jesus' saying, 'Judge not, and you will not be judged.' Beyond its moral implications, familiar to all, there is a Zen dimension to this word of the Gospel. Only when this Zen dimension is grasped will the moral bearing of it be fully clear."[7]

What Merton speaks of as a "Zen dimension" suggests a direct experience of things as they are, before thought, before the arising of what we usually consider to be the "self." Only the practice of sustained, prayerful presence and attention can unlock the deep "moral bearing" of Jesus' teaching about not judging. Efforts to put into practice the kind of not judging exemplified by the desert fathers in turn, deepen the possibilities for a prayer that is truly contemplative and all-embracing. The title of the present book refers to "Desert Wisdom" as it comments principally on texts from the desert fathers, but makes use of a wide variety of more recent writers and teachers characterized by a similar radicality, including a few Zen sources. Merton himself was among the first to note a certain kinship between the desert fathers and Zen.[8] What he refers to in this passage as the Zen dimension of not judging is present in Christian sources as well, and its recovery offers a ray of hope and inspiration in a polarized world.

[7] Thomas Merton, *Zen and the Birds of Appetite* (New York: New Directions, 1968), 6.

[8] Thomas Merton, *Wisdom in the Desert* (New York: New Directions, 1960), 9.

CHAPTER ONE

Mercy

> "Judge not": Christ himself does not judge. He is our judgment. Suffering innocence is the measure. Judgment; perspective. In this sense all judgment judges him who forms it. Not to judge. This is not indifference or abstention, it is transcendent judgment, the imitation of that divine judgment which is not possible for us.
>
> —Simone Weil, *Gravity and Grace*

"There was a man who had two sons" (Luke 15:11). In Jesus' best-known parable the two sons exaggerate and parody different sides of the father's character. The elder son is over-responsible, stiff, and righteous, where the father is stable, mature, and grounded. The younger son is reckless and sensual where the father is spontaneous, warm, and expressive. Locked in long-simmering rivalry the two sons push each other further out into more and more extreme parodies of qualities that are balanced and integrated in the father. Perhaps the elder son's habit of harsh and stingy judgment is part of why the younger son ran off—and part of the father's sympathy for the younger man. The more judgmental the elder son, the more reckless the younger. Over-controlling parent and sullen, surly teen:

types that often chase each other in circles, in our hearts and in the world around us.

Some speculate that the reason the father is watching anxiously for the son and so detects him while still a long way off, and the reason he's so demonstrative in his reception—the kiss, the robe, the banquet—is that the local villagers would have stoned the boy who had brought such dishonor on them by his scandalous behavior. The father had to head them off and assure them all that he was taking the injury on himself freely and absolving it. The lavish feast was a way to placate and reconcile the local people who would see themselves as sharing in the great dishonor brought upon the father by his son.

The younger son's response to this surprise display of warmth is to stammer out a few wooden lines from his hastily prepared script. By so free and gratuitous a display of compassion, the father hopes to awaken a gratuitous response in kind. In effect the father shows the younger son the generosity of which the son's prodigality is the parody. The son is overwhelmed. He doesn't know how to receive such compassion or what it means, how to receive it with his elder brother full of wrath lurking just outside the door.

In the Buddhist scriptures also there is a kind of parable of the lost son. In this story at a key point the wealthy father sees his (desperately poor) son who fails to recognize the father. Because he knows the son would feel unworthy of his kindness, the father arranges for the son to work for him, promoting him slowly up through the ranks, building trust between them and self-respect in the son, before at last revealing his identity, and entrusting to the young man his rightful inheritance. In Jesus' story, however expressive and unconditional the father's welcome, it will take time, perhaps many years, before the truth of this love will seep through the stiff armor of the younger son's fear and shame.

The elder son is hard at work in the field and hears the music and dancing from a distance. The eldest son would be expected at such a public gathering and his absence considered deeply insulting. "Listen! For all these years I have been working like a slave for you, and I have never disobeyed your command; yet you have never given me even a young goat to celebrate with my friends . . ." Who asked this son to work "like a slave," we might wonder. Did such a father operate by issuing "commands"? How could he imagine that such a generous father, who has divided his substance between his sons while still alive ("all that is mine is yours"), would deny him a goat? Did he really want to celebrate? Did he have "friends"?

The father, though he was in the form of a noble paterfamilias, emptied himself, taking the form of a suppliant, going out to his eldest son to plead with him. He put aside his paternal dignity: first in running out to receive the prodigal and then, in an even more piercing move, to persuade the elder son. Far from stoning the first son and disowning the second, the father, just as he shared out his wealth, empties himself of all status, of all regard for his dignity, and works to reconcile the brothers. In line with the words from Weil above, he suffers in innocence and so becomes the measure, the non-judgment by which the two sons can judge themselves. As Weil writes: "We must not judge. We must be like the Father in heaven who does not judge: by him beings judge themselves. We must let all beings come to us, and leave them to judge themselves. We must be a balance. Then we shall not be judged, having become an image of the true judge who does not judge."[1]

[1] Simone Weil, *Gravity and Grace*, trans. Emma Crawford and Mario von der Ruhr (New York: Routledge, 2003), 93.

Weil distinguishes elsewhere between the "good" that is merely social virtue, little more than the flipside of evil, and the absolute, "No one is good but God alone" (see Mark 10:18). The father in the parable gives expression to this transcendent good, not by floating above the fray, coldly indifferent, but by his willingness to suffer, to empty and humble himself. His peace is not the absence of conflict but a stable presence within it. His equanimity is not unfeeling but able to bear tension, unwilling to force a premature resolution. He is powerful in his weakness, humility, and patience, his non-judgment. Both sons, by contrast, judge one another and their father.

It's easy to imagine the younger son becoming more and more rebellious as the elder grows more self-righteous. He plays the role projected onto him all too readily and substantiates his older brother's role as policeman. He reduces him to his worst trait, in effect, judges him for judging. He sees his father too through the lens of his own shame. Confronted with his father's mercy he awkwardly mutters his scripted remarks, still imagining that such an evidently generous father could install him as a hired servant. The elder son views the younger as likewise defined by and reduced to his fault. He sees the father through the lens of his own stinginess: "I have been working like a slave . . . yet you have never given me even a young goat." The elder son compares himself to the younger.

The father by contrast insists on treating each of his sons precisely as sons, even when they effectively disown the role. By lavish, gratuitous love he seeks to awaken his likeness in each of them. His faithfulness creates, restores, and augments the bond between father and son and between the brothers. Where each of the sons clings to a sense of himself built over and against the other, the father is stubbornly with and for each son, just as he is, risking all to awaken a resonance, the light of their true nature as sons, unique expressions of his likeness.

This transformation doesn't happen once and for all in a flash. Or at least it happens both in a flash and in a gradual lifelong deepening. Even if the father's kindness breaks through the defenses of his sons it will take many years before the full reality of his goodness and their own potential is realized. The types of the elder and younger brother are echoed in the story of the repentant woman (Luke 7:36-50), with Simon akin to the elder brother, the woman like the younger son, and Jesus in the place of the father. In contrast to the prodigal's stiff, rehearsed apology, the woman is passionate and expressive in her sorrow. Where the elder brother is offstage when the younger returns, here the woman, a public sinner, dares to venture into the home of a professional religious she can expect will judge her harshly. The "faith" that "saved" her is expressed by her intensely vulnerable display of sorrow for her sin. Jesus' words, "Your sins are forgiven," which his adversaries interpret as performative ("I forgive you") can be read as a statement of fact: "Expressing such love, even in the face of harsh judgment, it's clear you've been forgiven by God." Jesus gently but firmly puts Simon in his place and responds with kindness to the woman.

If readers of these stories tend most often to identify with the younger son and the repentant woman, recalling times when they've fallen away and experienced forgiveness; and while some may find courage to recognize their own tendency to judge in the figures of the older brother and Simon, the challenge, it seems to me, is to take the place of the father between his sons, Jesus between Simon and the repentant woman. Each of us is inclined to exaggerate and distort the image of God within us in one or another direction: surly and hedonistic or stingy and righteous. In most of us these two chase each other around in circles. Hung over after a night of excess we berate ourselves so fiercely we set out on another bender as the only way to relieve the pressure. But the father does not seek defensively to appease or mollify the elder son. Nor does he react to the implied guilt trip by permissiveness, excusing away the younger son's actions. He doesn't engage the elder son's complaint directly but resets the focus on the grave peril the younger son faced and the joy of his return.

The word of God awakens an open space within us, a field where these warring contraries can abide . . . without judgment or a race to resolution, a non-dual space of not judging. It's just such a space the contemplative seeks to cultivate in prayer, a space where we can "let all beings come to us, and leave them to judge themselves. We must be a balance. Then we shall not be judged, having become an image of the true judge who does not judge."

The Gratuity of Grace

The repentant woman can love in such a generous and expressive way, in such a vulnerable way, in the presence of her accuser, only in response to the boundlessly gratuitous love of God. Because she's been forgiven much, she loves much. Her repentance was not a condition for this forgiveness any more than Jesus first required tax collectors and sinners to reform their lives before he would eat with them. This is what so scandalized the Pharisees. As St. Bernard wrote: "Love needs no cause beyond itself, nor does it demand fruits; it is its own purpose. I love because I love; I love that I may love."[2] God loves because he is love. The

[2] Bernard of Clairvaux, *On the Song of Songs IV*, trans. Irene Edmonds, CF 40 (Collegeville, MN: Liturgical Press, 1980), 184.

Good diffuses itself and can't do otherwise. God makes his sun shine and rain fall on good and bad alike. He is light in which there is no darkness.

If we say that God loves gratuitously *hoping* to evoke a similarly gratuitous love, this is not to place a condition or expect return payment, but an invitation to become who we are in the image of God: "Love is the only one of the motions of the soul, of its sense and affections, in which the creature can respond to its Creator, even if not as an equal, and repay his favor in some similar way." As Bernard explains shortly thereafter, "Although the creature loves less, being a lesser being, yet if it loves with its whole heart, nothing is lacking, for it has given all." God loves gratuitously hoping to awaken a gratuitous response, not for his own good, in which case his love would not be gratuitous, but rather, "he desires nothing but to be loved, since he loves us for no other reason than to be loved, for he knows that those who love him are blessed in their very love."[3]

While fear of punishment or self-interest might prompt us to do the right thing in the short-term, Bernard insists that lasting conversion of heart comes only from the experience of unconditional love. "Love moves us freely and it makes us free";[4] there is no trace of coercion. In going to the cross, the supremely free, supremely gratuitous act of love, God in Christ loves without remainder, hoping against hope to awaken a similar quality of love in human hearts; not because he needs it but because for us to love freely is to flourish.

[3] Bernard, *Song of Songs IV*, 184.

[4] See Bernard of Clairvaux, *On Loving God*, trans. Robert Walton, CF 13B (Collegeville, MN: Cistercian Publications, 1973), which translates, "Moving us freely, it makes us spontaneous."

Developing a familiar monastic scheme, Bernard speaks of three basic stages on the way. A slave fears God and because he is slavish imagines God is harsh and punitive. A hireling operates from self-interest and so imagines God to work likewise *quid pro quo*. One who has become a son, however, knows the father loves freely. Still, the love of the son does not eradicate the fear and self-interest of the slave and the hireling but takes up and transforms them, setting free the good energies trapped in these constricted modes of expression such that fear becomes reverence and self-interest an intelligent care for one's true well-being. Bernard adds to the triad of slave, hireling, son, the role of bride. Here the gratuitous character of a mature love that is mutual and free comes to complete fruition.

Like the slave, merchant, and even son, the roles of younger and older son in Jesus' parable are not genuine selves, but personified dispositions fixed over and against another. The elder son identifies as judge and the younger son as rebel. Locked in rivalry, they double down on these identifications. But the younger son also judges his older brother as an uptight moralistic hypocrite and the elder rebels against his father (by refusing to come in to the feast) in a way that would have been even more insulting than the younger son's departure.

Only the father can express himself in a way that is fully personal. He moves from zero, in a kind of free space, able to go in any direction, choosing to humble and empty himself, concerned only for the good of his sons. In contrast to the "self" fashioned over against another that characterizes the older and younger son, the freedom of the father arises as a kind of no-self. He has no stake in anything and nothing to defend. He is so at home in himself that he pours out all over, gives himself away without trying.

So the true self, our being in the image of God, can be thought of as a kind of "nothingness." In *The Book of Spiri-*

tual Poverty, for instance, the author speaks of the human spirit "raised above all images and all faculties into the bareness of God's being," where it grasps at last the dignity of its own true nature and is joined to God in spirit. "This being joined to God means nothing other than that the spirit goes out of itself according to its createdness and casts itself into a pure nothingness. And that nothingness is the divine image which has been imprinted in the soul and which remains there and cannot be destroyed."[5] We are like God insofar as we are "nothing" that can be named or comprehended, a nothingness expressed as gratuitous love in response to gratuitous love. "Love moves us freely and it makes us free."[6] When both God and his image are nothing, there is no object, no obstacle, only the rapture of bride and groom.

The two sons, like all rivals, are locked in comparison. The story of Mary and Martha is conventionally read in terms of "contemplative" versus "active" life. But the problem is not that Martha is serving, or even that she's busy and somewhat harried. Rather, she compares herself to Mary: "Don't you care that I'm doing all this work while Mary just sits there?" She calls attention to and valorizes her own work while judging Mary for her idleness. The story could be told the other way. Mary could be listening to Jesus while Martha works and Mary could say, "Don't you care that Martha is bustling about while I'm here reverently listening? Tell her to give up her way and take up mine . . ." The desert fathers will repeatedly underline the importance of not comparing ourselves to others.

[5] *The Rhineland Mystics*, trans. Oliver Davies (New York: Crossroad, 1990), 119.

[6] "Moving us freely, it [love] makes us spontaneous." Bernard of Clairvaux, *On Loving God*, trans. Robert Walton, in *Treatises II*, CF 13 (Collegeville, MN: Cistercian Publications, 1973), 110.

Sacrifice

Bernard writes that God is "neither offended by our sins nor placated by our penance."[7] To grasp this pulls the plug on a certain kind of "mythological Catholicism" built on the projections of the slave and the hireling. In the ancient world "sacrifice" had the sense of "exchange," crudely: I throw my daughter in the volcano so that god must bestow a fruitful harvest. Beginning in the first covenant then definitively in Christ, the living God turns this inside out and upside down. He takes the initiative and gives himself freely, hoping against hope, as we've seen, to awaken a like response.

The story of Abraham and Isaac is usually read to mean that Abraham was heroic because he was willing to sacrifice Isaac. Abraham had received a free gift and since there is no such thing as a free gift he assumed he must give back what he'd been given. But it was from just this mentality, and an ambient culture where child sacrifice was common, that God was leading Abraham out. Suppose then that it was Abraham alone who imagined God wanted him to sacrifice Isaac. The living God intervened, distinguishing himself from the surrounding gods by his free gift and his abhorrence of child sacrifice. Abraham then shows faith by *not* sacrificing Isaac but accepting the free gift of God. Then with all his familiar cultural and religious bearings swept away, Abraham set out into a vast desert, "not knowing where he was going" (Heb 11:8).

Although child sacrifice, at least in the form Abraham knew, is not so common today, the basic dynamic endures. Imagine, for instance, an alcoholic or drug addict trying to

[7] Bernard of Clairvaux, *Sentences* 124.3, in *The Parables and The Sentences*, trans. Michael Casey and Francis R. Swietek, CF 55 (Collegeville, MN: Cistercian Publications, 1991), 436.

get sober. He tries everything, treatment programs, counseling, but nothing works. His marriage falls apart and he loses his job. He tries and tries but can't break free. At last he hits bottom and gives up. Amazingly he finds the sensation of fierce craving lifted. He starts to go to 12 Step meetings and get his life back together. Although his liberation was in no way the result of his own effort, before long he begins to tell himself that it's because he goes to six meetings a week and the gym each night that he's finally back on track. We desperately want, or imagine we want, for salvation to be based on something we control. Even when it means doing violence to ourselves, when we must "sacrifice" what we love, it seems safer than reliance on the free gift of an unknown power.

The father in the story is not "offended" by the sin of his younger son. He throws his dignity to the wind in relief and joy that the boy has returned. He is not placated by the offer to work as his slave. He holds a banquet and honors the son, embracing him with warmth and affection. It is the elder son, the rival in the shadows, who is offended, who demands revenge. William Blake wrote: "Every Religion that Preaches Vengeance for Sin is the Religion of the Enemy and Avenger and not the Forgiver of Sin and their God is Satan." It is a great tragedy that the gospel of mercy has so often been highjacked by "Nobodaddy," Blake's name for this religious superego, and the free gift of grace overshadowed by the mythological superstructure of "sacrifice."[8] Jesus goes to the cross in complete freedom as a supreme

[8] My understanding of sacrifice, violence, and rivalry in these pages is indebted to the thought of the French theorist René Girard. Girard is best known for his writings on the scapegoat mechanism and the mimetic nature of human desire. One helpful starting place for exploring his work is René Girard, *I See Satan Fall like Lightning*, trans. James G. Williams (Maryknoll, NY: Orbis, 2001).

expression of gratuitous love and what we hear instead is the guilt-trip of a resentful parent: "I gave up so much for you, can you not at least ____?" It's tragic that the very faith that leads the way beyond guilt, violence, and judgment has so often been tainted, if not outright highjacked, by the spirit of the Accuser.

Stop Judging

The challenge in the parable of the prodigal son is to be like the father. The father does not reconcile in himself the dispositions represented by the sons through negotiation, adjusting back and forth, a little more reckless, a bit less judgmental, now more merciful, now a bit more just. He simply moves from zero. He is guided only by love for each son; he addresses himself to each son as he truly is, a true likeness of the father, and overlooks the distorted parody each presents. He doesn't even discriminate between good and bad. He makes his rain fall and sun shine on good and bad alike. He wholeheartedly allows and embraces what is contrary, what resists his love. In this way he is the perfect icon of the heavenly Father who allows the weeds and the wheat to grow together. The one soil nourishes the life of both and trusts that the good will prevail. The father, like the Father, is with and for all. "Love your enemies and pray for those who persecute you, so that you may be children of your Father in heaven" (Matt 5:44-45); not that you may bring about this or that outcome but in order to express your true nature as a distinct likeness of God in the world.

Whether the father succeeds in reconciling the sons or not, or only quite imperfectly, he is free. For righteousness to surpass that of "the scribes and Pharisees," it must be interior. To speak in wrath already subjects us to fiery Gehenna. As we judge others, so we experience ourselves to be judged. As we judge ourselves harshly, so we judge others. The only way out: Jesus said to his disciples, "Be merciful, just as your Father is merciful. Do not judge, and you will not be judged; do not condemn, and you will not be condemned. Forgive, and you will be forgiven; give, and it will be given to you. A good measure, pressed down, shaken together, running over, will be put into your lap, for the measure you give will be the measure you get back" (Luke 6:36-38). To act (positively) with and for corresponds with the (negative) command to stop judging. Psychologically, as long as we are criticizing, diagnosing, passing judgment, we will at some level be bracing for counterattack, where if we lead with empathy we remain secure and grounded. We give and receive mercy through the same opening. It's created by the free gift of forgiveness from God then widened by passing on that gift, or narrowed by judging. It's one "measure." So like the repentant woman in Luke, the one who has been forgiven much loves much.

Unconditional Love

This story of the Japanese poet Ryokan provides another image of not judging and a prodigal son. Ryokan's nephew Umanosuke

> was squandering the family money for his own personal pleasure. Asked by Umanosuke's mother to give him advice, Ryokan went to the Tachibana-ya. He stayed there for three days but said nothing. On his departure for his hermitage, Ryokan stood at the porch, called for Umanosuke, and asked him to tie the strings of his straw sandals. Umanosuke's mother, who stood behind the screen, was hoping that Ryokan would give him some strong advice. Umanosuke didn't understand why Ryokan had asked him to do such an unusual thing but followed his request. As he bent to the

> task, he felt something wet on his neck. He was surprised and looked up. He saw Ryokan's eyes full of tears. At that moment he felt repentance for his wrongdoings. Ryokan stood up and left without a word.[9]

Sin can only be known in the moment it's forgiven. Otherwise we could never bear to face it squarely. It's the awareness of the full extent of our misery in the same moment that we realize we are loved, unconditionally, just as we are. Knowing we are loved just as we are, while seeing keenly and with fresh eyes the nature of our fault, is what prompts us to want to change, from within and freely. As Bernard said, you can compel the slave to change by fear, or the hireling by self-interest, but it won't last and the change will be superficial. Only when we know that we don't need to change in order to be loved do we want to change . . . not to earn what's already been freely given but from gratitude. Gratuity in response to gratuity.

A similar dynamic occurs in a story from the desert. A visiting monk makes off with a beautiful edition of the complete scriptures belonging to Abba Anastasius. The thief tries to sell the book and the book dealer takes the volume to the same Anastasius to have it appraised. The abba says simply that, yes, it is worth the price being asked. When the book dealer reports this to the thief and that he is willing to purchase the book, the monk declares that it's no longer for sale. Struck to the heart he returns to Anastasius and repents. The abba invites him to keep the book but the monk insists that if he keeps the book he will have no peace. He then becomes a disciple of Anastasius and freely devotes the rest of his life to serving him. Anastasius would have been fully within his rights to claim the book when

[9] Kazuaki Tanahashi, *Sky Above, Great Wind: The Life and Poetry of Zen Master Ryokan* (Boulder, CO: Shambhala, 2012), 5.

approached by the dealer but his more creative and generous response inspired the profound transformation of a wayward monk.[10]

We use the expression "unconditional love" too lightly. If we really grasped what it meant—no way to earn or lose the boundless free gift of love, of God's being with and for us—it would completely change our lives. But what if the nephew remained unmoved? Is there not a time for "tough love"? Someone acting like Ryokan, like the father of the prodigal son, simply expresses who and how they are. There is no attachment to a given outcome. He is not trying to coerce, to guilt-trip the other into a, however lightly, forced conversion. He leaves the other completely free. In fact it's just that respect for the other's freedom that strikes them to the heart.

Certainly there is a time and a way to protect the innocent from harm, situations where other approaches may be prudent. But whether in the personal or political sphere we are far more addicted to force than we realize; and what outcome best serves "justice"? We might consider: if some atrocity were carried out against someone I love, would I rather the attacker spent life in jail and went to their grave without a trace of remorse, or that without time in jail they were struck to the heart and for the rest of their lives saw ever more clearly, and mourned for, the suffering they'd caused? So often when we speak of balancing "justice" and "mercy" we're imagining God as some moody parent lurching arbitrarily between permissive indulgence and petty revenge. But in God there's no difference between justice and mercy. Nothing's more just than his mercy, nothing more merciful than his justice.

[10] Thomas Merton, *The Wisdom of the Desert: Sayings from the Desert Fathers of the Fourth Century* (New York: New Directions, 1970), 30–31.

"Repentance" here is not something we do to earn or qualify for forgiveness but the sign we've become aware that our sins have already been forgiven. Our part is simply to consent. False repentance leaves us spinning our wheels in self-hatred. We don't really change or go forward. With true repentance we may feel very bitter remorse—we see with icy clarity the harm we've caused, the extent of our selfishness and cruelty—but have a sense of hope, even excitement, and feel empowered to change. We see what was wrong and feel energized to set it right. The judgment of the word, "sharper than any two-edged sword . . . able to judge the thoughts and intentions of the heart" (Heb 4:12), even as we're pierced with compunction empowers and energizes. It's the false judge, the Accuser within, who breeds despair and self-hatred.

A text in the book of Wisdom (2:12-22) presents the scheming of the wicked against the just man in a way that foreshadows the attack on Jesus by his accusers: "He became to us a reproof of our thoughts; / the very sight of him is a burden to us, / because his manner of life is unlike that of others, / and his ways are strange. / We are considered by him as something base . . ." If we imagine these words on the lips of those who opposed the ministry of Jesus, how much of this harsh judgment they perceive is the reflection of their own violence, of the way they are themselves judging Christ? They might instead have been challenged and encouraged by Jesus' witness like his disciples. "Thus they reasoned, but they were led astray, / for their wickedness blinded them."

As he approaches the cross, Jesus certainly pulls no punches in confronting his attackers, but how often he sat at table with them, bearing patiently their attempts to test and to trap him in speech. His own image for the approach he takes to the Pharisees is the father of the prodigal son going out to plead with the older brother. Like the Pharisees, the son, too, feels he's been wronged and offended by the father. Because Jesus' opponents were judging harshly, they felt themselves to be harshly judged. "The measure you give will be the measure you get back." As in a favorite verse of Bernard, from Sirach (14:5), "If they are mean to themselves, to whom will they be generous?"

In the parable of the unjust steward, a desperate man is gratuitously forgiven all then immediately turns on an underling and demands repayment. Why? It seems to me that he hasn't really received the free gift from his master. Instead he feels humiliated by the largesse shown him and to shore up his self-respect has to intimidate another. While this example is drastic, the basic dynamic is all too common. We fail to register the grace we've received, to assimilate the gift and allow it to flower. We've "had the experience but missed the meaning."[11] Very often we are looking for some new grace, some new or different experience when we already have all we need, and have simply to unpack and digest what we've already received. A deepening spiritual practice demands sustained, unjudging attention to experience without evading or glossing over it. If the unjust steward had been present to the master's gratuitous kindness and his own relief, and not preoccupied by shame and status, gratitude could have emerged, supplanting fear. We can never underestimate our need to soak in and savor, to marinate in divine mercy.

Oddly, in a word play the first Cistercians were fond of, the more honestly we attend to the reality of our misery (*miseria*) the more we perceive the far greater reality of

[11] T. S. Eliot, "The Dry Salvages," in *Four Quartets* (London: Faber & Faber, 1941).

God's mercy (*misericordia*) . . . and vice versa. In a memorable image St. Isaac of Syria says that as a handful of sand thrown into the sea, so are the sins of all humanity compared to the ocean of divine mercy. We obsess over and fixate on the few grains of sand that comprise our guilt and fail to see the breathtaking beauty of that infinitely vast ocean of grace. We must learn to lift our gaze, again and again, from the handful of sand to the sea. The reality of God, his goodness, is so astounding, so great a cause of joy, that our faults drop into perspective. Our sins are no obstacle to grace. Only our stubborn fixation on our sins, our attachment to a view of ourselves as hateful, hinders the healing flow.

It can happen that with time a kind of Copernican revolution occurs where our sins, and in fact our entire selves, dim in importance before the reality of divine goodness that completely fills the horizon. Simone Weil expresses this, a bit shockingly: "Joy within God. Perfect and infinite joy really exists within God. My participation can add nothing to it, my non-participation can take nothing from the reality of this perfect and infinite joy. Of what importance is it then whether I am to share in it or not? Of no importance whatever."[12] It is enough that God is God. In the first testament, when Jacob learns that his son Joseph, once presumed dead, is in fact still living, he exclaims, "It is enough for me that Joseph is alive." The Cistercian writer Guerric of Igny makes these words his own in relation to the risen presence of Christ after his brutal death: "It is enough for me that Jesus is still alive."[13] Whether I live or die, whether I am a sinner or the greatest saint, what matters is the all-consuming reality of divine goodness.

[12] Weil, *Gravity and Grace*, 37.

[13] Guerric of Igny, *Liturgical Sermons*, vol. 2, trans. Monks of Mt. St. Bernard Abbey, CF 32 (Collegeville, MN: Cistercian Publications, 1971), 84.

Original Innocence

If even our actual sins, acts of selfishness we to some degree freely chose and for which we bear responsibility, are grains of sand before the ocean of mercy, how much more are the wounds, flaws, and trauma we bear through no fault of our own met with an abundance of healing and mercy. "Original sin" means we are born into a world of damaged relationality.[14] Imagine a baby born addicted to cocaine because her mother was using during pregnancy. The baby has done absolutely nothing to "deserve" the ensuing pain. She is totally innocent of any action for which she could be held responsible ("actual sin"). The conditions into which she's born and the trauma she suffers set her up to act in certain (harmful) ways as she reaches maturity.

The desert fathers speak of that underlying conditioning in terms of the "passions," deep-seated fears and defenses, obsessions and compulsions that color and shape the kinds of trouble we're prone to. Often, we feel far greater shame over these wounds that came about through no fault of our own than we do guilty for acts for which we are actually responsible. Without healing the underlying wounds we can't effectively address our sins, because the way we sin is usually a misguided attempt to medicate those very wounds. The trouble is, wounds left to fester and atrophy are often so sore, so hard to look at and feel, and the "medication" comes so close to working, that we're disinclined to face them.

To face the wound means inhabiting our original innocence, our profound vulnerability, and acknowledging the pain of what happened. In this original innocence we are like Christ, who suffered through no fault of his own,

[14] What follows draws on Neil Ormerod's account of original sin in Neil Ormerod, *Creation, Grace, and Redemption* (Maryknoll: Orbis, 2007), 79–84.

who chose to willingly take responsibility for the world's guilt, and to mystically unite himself to its anguish. Because he has "borne our sufferings" in this way we can experience the ocean in every grain of sand, every experience of misery can become the locus of a healing so profound we may even come to count it a "happy fault," to be grateful for what we've suffered as the occasion through which we've known such liberating grace.

Frequently guilt and sin are confused with innocent suffering. In the New Testament we see this repeatedly. Of the man born blind: "Who sinned, this man or his parents . . . ?" (John 9:2). Again and again Jesus restores the stigmatized and excluded to the community, heals, and when needed, forgives, and challenges the religious professionals of his time so eager "to pile burdens on others while failing to lift a finger to help" (see Matt 23:4). Jesus opens up the space of the interior and addresses sin at its root.

What of Jesus' own relation to sin? He is said to have suffered and been like us in all things but without sin. One way to read this: Jesus suffered "trauma" like the rest of us, when, for instance, he was forced to migrate in desperate and violent circumstances as a child—but somehow never closed in around the wound, never developed the kinds of defenses the rest of us do, or at least, was able to let these go when they'd served their purpose. Somehow, we might imagine, Jesus was able to radically own and express his profound vulnerability, our profound vulnerability, without turning away, without glossing over, medicating, or otherwise seeking to escape from suffering. He was free from sin because there was no basis in him for sin, nowhere for it to get a hold. Because the wounds were held open to the healing grace of the Father, because of the singular graces received by Mary and Joseph, the wounds were not allowed to fester and didn't become infected as they do for us.

CHAPTER TWO

Peace

> There is perhaps no phenomenon which contains so much destructive feeling as "moral indignation," which permits envy or hate to be acted out under the guise of virtue.
>
> —Erich Fromm, *Man for Himself: An Inquiry into the Psychology of Ethics*

Earlier we read this quintessential saying on not judging: "Abba Poemen said to Abba Joseph, 'Tell me how to become a monk.' He said, 'If you want to find rest here below, and hereafter, in all circumstances say, Who am I? and do not judge anyone.' "[1] Asked about how to become a monk, Abba Joseph replies, "If you want to find rest . . ." suggesting an equivalence: a monk is one who has sought and found rest—rest from the turmoil of life in the world, and in particular rest from the inner turmoil of the passions (*apatheia*). For the desert tradition, influenced by Stoicism, the passions are not emotions in general but by definition disordered and afflictive energies. The passion of "anger,"

[1] *The Sayings of the Desert Fathers: The Alphabetical Collection*, trans. Benedicta Ward, CS 59 (Collegeville, MN: Cistercian Publications, 1984), 102. Hereafter, *Sayings*.

for instance, has the sense of wrath and malice. The monk is one who seeks rest from his own programming, the pattern of ingrained reactivity by which he's triggered. This rest is not the abolition of the passions—they may go dormant to some degree, for a time, but remain below the surface—rather a monk finds peace in and through his inner turmoil, learning to deal wisely and gently with his conditioning over many years. "If you want to find rest" also implies a question: do you truly seek rest? Are you willing to do what it takes to find it?

Bernard of Clairvaux writes of sin as fundamentally arrogance, the attempt to claim for oneself a "glory" that belongs to God alone. Humility, by contrast, is more than content with the profound gift of peace God offers. Bernard addresses God: "I wish for peace, I yearn for it and for nothing more. The man who is not satisfied with peace is not satisfied with you. For you are our peace, you have made us both one. To be reconciled with you, to be reconciled with myself, this is necessary for me, and it suffices. For whenever you set me in opposition to you, I become a burden to myself."[2] Most of us need to exhaust ourselves and crash, repeatedly, before discovering in our heart of hearts that this peace that surpasses understanding is all we really want.

Abba Joseph speaks of seeking rest both here and in the life to come. It's striking that he thinks peace, a peace akin to that in heaven, is actually possible on earth. The way is simple and must be applied universally, "in all circumstances" without exception: "say, Who am I? and do not judge anyone." There are not some occasions where judging

[2] Bernard of Clairvaux, *On the Song of Songs I*, The Works of Bernard of Clairvaux, vol. 2, trans. Kilian Walsh, CF 4 (Collegeville, MN: Cistercian Publications, 1971), 91.

would be the better way. No extenuating circumstances, no *realpolitik* conditions demanding we bracket the gospel and act with violence from "necessity."

To apply the kind of not-judging Abba Joseph has in view is always the way. It involves two closely related steps: to ask, who is this "I" that would judge another? And by implication, who is this other, really, that I would judge? Once the accuser and accused alike are seen through as fictions, a residue generated by the heat of our indignation, it becomes impossible to judge. It's not so much a matter of willpower—we're sorely tempted to pass judgment but manage by a heroic effort not to—but rather we ask deeply, "Who am I?" Who is this I, right now, stirred up, accusatory, outraged? Is this really "me"? What causes the identification of these powerful feelings with me?

That we are not our thoughts and that it is not for sinful thoughts that we are condemned, but only for making use of them, is a crucial teaching of the fathers.[3] The accused other, the converse of my own livid accuser, is likewise unreal, a drastic simplification, a stereotype and not an accurate intuition of a real human being. Asking the question, "Who am I?" is critical to non-judgment because we judge precisely in order to establish a sense of self over and against another. We get a boost, a fleeting sense of empowerment . . . but it's based on a mirage.

The saying reminds us of our familiar expression, "Who am I to judge?" This carries the sense that I too am a weak, fallible human being so not in a position to judge. It still involves a comparison of oneself with another. To ask in all circumstances "Who am I?" prevents the sense of self

[3] See for instance, Thomas Merton, *The Wisdom of the Desert: Sayings from the Desert Fathers of the Fourth Century* (New York: New Directions, 1970), 45.

formed by judging from congealing into something solid. We are kept off-balance and make room for unknowing. We call into question the self that would judge, that would compare itself with another. I once read a book by a criminal psychiatrist who studied the most violent criminals, men (usually) who committed sudden, gruesome murders without apparent motive. What he learned was that at root, these murderers had a bottomless dread of disappearing, and the grisly killing was a desperate way of inscribing themselves into life and history, of making a mark, signing their name. The same impulse perhaps lies at the root of even superficial judgments: the desire to erase the other and inscribe my self prompted by a deep-seated fear of vanishing.

Colossians speaks of a self renewed in "the image of its creator." The "old self" is characterized as Jew or Greek, slave or free, this over and against that, where the new self is a reality in which "Christ is all and in all" (Col 3:10-11). The new self lives with the life of another: "It is no longer I who live but it is Christ who lives in me" (Gal 2:20); it is with and for all as Christ is all and in all. It lives with the same life and begins from this union. Far from an elision or abolition of differences, rootedness in the shared ground of communion allows the full articulation of each in their irreducible uniqueness.

In the story, recounted earlier, of the brothers who see a woman enter the cell of a fellow monk, the abba stomps off loudly as though infected by the same contagious persecutory fervor that infects the group. In fact he sees in the outrage of his monks a greater threat to the well-being of the community than the poor behavior of an individual. That he responds so immediately in this way, overcoming the strong pressure to join with the mob, suggests a cultivated distrust of the accusatory crowd. He appears to go along with them, however, shouting loudly as he approaches in feigned anger, giving the monk and his amour time to hide. In the brother caught in the act, the monks do not see their brother, a fragile, fallible human being who has fallen in a moment of weakness, but a malicious transgressor, acting on the desires they disown in themselves. The self that might serve as a basis for empathy is quickly lost in the mob and its breathless desire to humiliate and exclude the brother who has broken a rule. In every lynch mob, the victim who is punished involves a collective projection. Innocent or guilty, the accused always represents more than an individual like any other who has committed a crime. He bears the weight of the lynch mob's shadow.

The abba who responds with such alacrity and discretion demonstrates what Samuel Wells calls "overacceptance." Arguing that Christian moral life is more like improvisation and less like working from a preset script, Wells looks at the drama games practiced by actors in training for insight into moral action. In skits demanding improvisation a player can either block or accept the cues offered by a partner. The skilled actor not only goes along with the scenario sketched by his partner but "overaccepts," takes on the cue with a kind of wild generosity spinning it in some new unforeseen and imaginative direction.[4]

Such ability demands great spontaneity, courage, and freedom of spirit. In the moral sphere, it's the kind of approach required to deescalate and redirect a group under the sway of the Accuser. It's the approach taken by Jesus when confronted with the adulterous woman, and supremely in his path to the cross. Without missing a beat, the abba rolls along with and appears to amplify the persecutory fervor of the mob, wading into the situation with a view to "turn"

[4] Samuel Wells, *Improvisation: The Drama of Christian Ethics* (Grand Rapids, MI: Brazos, 2004).

it in such a way that both the accused and the accusers may learn what they need to. This is what it looks like when someone has deeply internalized the practice: in all circumstances ask, "Who am I? and do not judge anyone."

Numerous scripture passages ask versions of the question, "Who am I to judge?" Paul, for instance, in Romans: "Who are you to pass judgment on slaves of another?" (Rom 14:4); or James: "There is one lawgiver and judge who is able to save and to destroy. So who, then, are you to judge your neighbor?" (Jas 4:12). Jesus' teaching and parables constantly challenge us to defer judgment to God: the weeds are allowed to grow alongside the wheat, the net includes all the fish, good and bad alike. For one thing, one who is just now may fall tomorrow, and one who is fallen now may rise.

In another saying from the desert: "Whenever his thoughts urged him to pass judgment on something which he saw, he would say to himself, 'Agathon, it is not your business to do that.' Thus his spirit was always recollected."[5] As above one asks, Who am I? "in all circumstances," so here Agathon determines that it is not his place to judge "whenever," in each instance, he's tempted to. Because he was recollected, he was able to adopt this posture, and because he did so, he was able to remain recollected. From an inner space of presence and attention, it's harder to slip into rancor. Recollection is itself a space of non-judgment in which whatever thoughts and passions arise are allowed to come to light. In another place it is said that a certain abba held forth all day in spiritual conversation for the benefit of many and never broke silence, while another remained alone but because he judged his brother in his heart failed to keep silence.

[5] *Sayings*, 23.

Agathon also said: "A man who is angry, even if he were to raise the dead, is not acceptable to God."[6] Again, we must underline that what the desert fathers mean by "anger" and "judgment" is something that by definition is skewed by passion, wrathful and condemnatory. Just how challenging the struggle with anger can be is attested by Abba Ammonas, who said, "I have spent fourteen years in Scetis asking God night and day to grant me the victory over anger."[7] His tremendous and focused perseverance is dedicated to asking God for victory as he knows he can't attain it on his own. Such asking fosters the humility that alone makes way for "the victory over anger."

In one exchange, "A brother questioned Abba Poemen saying, 'What does it mean to be angry with your brother without a cause?' He said, 'If your brother hurts you by his arrogance and you are angry with him because of it, that is getting angry without cause. If he plucks out your right eye and cuts off your right hand, and you get angry with him, you are angry without cause. But if he separates you from God, then be angry with him.' "[8] This passage may refer to the threat of misleading teaching but it's also possible to ask, can another person actually separate us from God? "Who will separate us from the love of Christ?" (Rom 8:35). That may be the point. There is no cause for anger. If there were, it would not be to defend our esteem or even our body, reacting in kind to hostility, but the prospect of separation from God. Our own anger and judgment, as the desert fathers understand them, are in fact what separate us from God and the one thing we ought to resist.

[6] *Sayings*, 23.

[7] *Sayings*, 26.

[8] *Sayings*, 184.

Are we then to get angry at our anger? Yes and no. In general, fighting the passions with the passions tends to backfire, like fighting the mind with the mind, or being anxious about our anxiety. However, if we find ourselves repeatedly and unfairly self-righteous and judgmental, we might be given the grace to form a firm resolve to humble ourselves and make a change: "anger" at our judging others in the sense of zeal to correct injustice. The danger is that we simply turn the same quality of harsh indignation on ourselves and so compound it. In social settings also, there is a perennial danger of the advocate turning into the accuser. Not to fall into this trap it's essential to keep in view that fundamentally we are all on the same side struggling with the passions, and the Accuser loves nothing more than to disperse our energies by turning us against each another.

One last saying on anger, from Abba Macarius: "If you reprove someone, you yourself get carried away by anger and you are satisfying your own passion; do not lose yourself, therefore, in order to save another."[9] We can see this perhaps in connection with the comments earlier on recollection. If we lose our composure and clarity in correcting another, even if we are successful in warning him away from his poor conduct, we would ourselves have fallen under its sway, our "correction" no more than a reaction in kind to the offender's own passionate behavior. Of course there are those entrusted with correcting others, and they may feel heated about the situation in which they need to speak out. This saying can serve as a kind of examen to sift what we're experiencing ahead of an intervention. Do we need more distance? Are we "on the war path," however rationalized?

As we will see more fully in later chapters the gift of which judgment is a distortion is spiritual discernment,

[9] *Sayings*, 131.

which is characterized by the ability to hold in view the passions activated within us, with a sense of how they skew our perspective. As Weil writes, "The presence of illusions which we have abandoned but which are still present in the mind is perhaps the criterion of truth."[10] Surely one of the reasons Jesus tells his disciples to bring other people in to mediate a conflict when it can't be resolved one on one is that it's so easy for us to fool ourselves. Just as we mustn't allow ourselves to be separated from God, we mustn't "lose ourselves" and surrender equanimity even (and perhaps especially) when we set out to save another person from his poor behavior.

"Life Is Round"

There's an expression, "Strong opinions, weakly held."[11] It's possible to believe the right thing in the wrong way or for the wrong reasons, which tends to discredit the truth in question. I take holding strong views weakly, or lightly, to mean that our very sense of identity is not invested in this or that articulation of a truth. We are willing to have our perspective broadened and challenged, trusting that truth will come to light with time. Insisting on our perspective in any given moment, we become playthings of the Accuser. A story in the *Sayings* describes two brothers who have lived together for many years with great harmony. Seeking to stir up discord, the enemy appears at their door, to one appearing like a dove, to another like a raven. Each insists on what they see to the point that a fistfight breaks out. After a few days they settle down and reconcile. "They

[10] Simone Weil, *Gravity and Grace*, trans. Emma Crawford and Mario von der Ruhr (New York: Routledge, 2003), 78.

[11] Attributed to Stanford professor Paul Saffo; at one time a trendy slogan in Silicon Valley, it is borrowed here for my own ends.

recognized that each of them had believed the bird to be what he had seen and recognized that their conflict came from the enemy. So they lived to the end without being separated."[12]

Our perception at any given moment is subject to correction and refinement and the more open we are to this process, aware that things are not always what they seem, the more easily we grow in truth. The brothers come to recognize that each of them sincerely, and understandably enough, believed the bird to be what it appeared to them to be. At the time, the possibility their brother might really be seeing something they could not didn't occur to them. Insisting that what they saw was how things "really" were allowed them to be duped. Other stories tell of monks who seem to see a brother committing sin but when they approach to verify discover only a haystack and some rags. The spirit of anger and judgment is tendentious and looks for evidence to confirm its skewed reading of events. If somebody wants to be scandalized they will easily enough find or create an occasion.

In the story about the woman entering the monk's cell the mob of accusing brothers both did and did not see what they thought they did. Although they apparently did see the brother getting too close with this woman, his act quickly assumed larger than life importance. He was seen as a poison that must be immediately spit out from the community. The abba's spontaneous trick has the effect of turning them back on themselves to ask again what it was they actually saw: a devious seducer or a brother caught in a moment of weakness?

As we've seen, when another person really gets under our skin it's often because something in their behavior

[12] *Sayings*, 157.

touches something we've disowned in ourselves. This is commonplace but no less difficult to see and work with. Weil again: "Why is the determination to fight against a prejudice a sure sign that one is full of it? Such a determination necessarily arises from an obsession. It constitutes an utterly sterile effort to get rid of it. In such a case the light of attention is the only thing which is effective, and it is not compatible with a polemical intention."[13]

To underline: the moral crusader filled with righteous indignation proceeds obsessively, not calmly or with clarity; and his efforts are sterile, ineffective, undermined by his own lack of self-awareness. Only contemplative attention that reflects things just as they are, like a mirror and without judging, can heal the passions. In the clear light of non-judging attention we can begin to own what we have projected onto others. We can take up our own cross, the burden of our wounds and conditioning, instead of tying up heavy burdens for others without lifting a finger to help. With time we can bear one another's burdens and so fulfill the law of Christ.

"A brother said to Abba Matoes: 'Give me a word.' He said to him, 'Restrain the spirit of controversy in yourself in everything, and weep, have compunction, for the time is drawing near.'"[14] Notice we're not to restrain the spirit of controversy in others so that we fall into judging others for being judgmental, but in ourselves; our own propensity to fight for the sake of fighting. Again the word is applied across the board, "in everything"; there's no occasion where indulging "the spirit of controversy" is fruitful. Weeping and compunction are appropriate when we've begun to own

[13] Weil, *Gravity and Grace*, 55.

[14] *Sayings*, 145.

the aspects of ourselves we dislike and tend to foist onto others.

When in the very next saying a brother asks despairingly, "What am I to do?" confessing that he can't seem to restrain himself from condemning others, he is told: "If you cannot contain yourself, flee into solitude. For this is a sickness. He who dwells with brethren must not be square, but round, so as to turn himself towards all." He goes on to say that he himself lives as a hermit out of weakness, not strength, and that the strong ones are those who bear the trials of life in community.[15]

If we can't restrain ourselves from judging, we need to step back and get distance. The image of becoming round instead of angular suggests displaying the same face to all, as the Father of Jesus who makes his rain fall and sun shine on everyone. Needless to say, that smoothening and rounding can only take place through real encounters with others; encounters that are often messy, awkward, and difficult. Our thinking is angular but as van Gogh once said, "Life is round."

Contemplative prayer is a space of nondiscrimination. It is not anti-intellectual but pre-reflective and clears the way for thought in harmony with life. The "light of attention" that Weil speaks of is incompatible with "a polemical intention," with the mind that busily sets this against that. Instead it rests simply with things as they are, with our experience, just as it is, without judging or changing anything. Spending time in this kind of stillness in which we are not "judging" in the basic sense of not pursuing discursive reflection undergirds the practice of "not-judging" in the moral sphere. We cultivate distance or space in which our rage and punitive fantasies can come to light, and the needs

[15] *Sayings*, 145.

below the anger be addressed. Remaining in stillness, what is not still, our restless mind and anxious passions, become visible.

"Abba Nilus said, 'Everything you do in revenge against a brother who has harmed you will come back to you at the time of prayer.' "[16] There's a natural feedback loop between our conduct through the day and our experience in prayer. If we act with mercy through the day our conscience will be still and it will be easier to rest in prayer, whereas if we're judging others it will come to light when we try to pray—not as some kind of punishment but because of this root "incompatibility" between prayerful attention and polemical intention. There is a converse saying of Nilus just after this one: "Whatever you have endured out of love of wisdom will bear fruit for you at the time of prayer."[17]

Nilus also said: "Prayer is the seed of gentleness and the absence of anger."[18] Again, this doesn't mean that angry and judgmental thoughts do not arise in prayer—just the opposite as we've seen. The quiet of prayer allows us to hear and attend to our thoughts, what we're really feeling, what's happening in our bodies, and so on. Because prayer allows room for anger to arise, before God, in quiet, it becomes a "seed of gentleness," the beginning, the first hint of a response to real or imagined injustice that is not reactive and obsessive but balanced and self-aware. Prayer involves an inner state of trust and surrender in which we allow all the sides of ourselves to come to light in the presence of unconditional love, of a Father who "knows what we need before we ask" and numbers every hair on our head.

[16] *Sayings*, 153.
[17] *Sayings*, 153.
[18] *Sayings*, 153–54.

When a brother asks Abba Agathon about sexual sin, the abba replies, "Go, cast your weakness before God and you shall find rest."[19] This seems almost like an abbreviation of Paul: "Do not be anxious about anything, but in everything by prayer and supplication with thanksgiving let your requests be made known to God. And the peace of God, which surpasses understanding, will guard your hearts and your minds in Christ Jesus" (Phil 4:6-7). We make known our need by becoming present to it ourselves, by allowing it into the light of divine presence. This is especially important in areas like sexual sin, around which there is often a great deal of shame and so a strong tendency to hide the wound and keep it buried in secrecy, where it will fester.

The desert fathers stress repeatedly the need to bring thoughts and passions to the light: to cast our weakness before God and to share our thoughts with a trusted mentor. The enemy is often portrayed tempting monks not to disclose the thoughts that burden them out of fear and shame. This saying of Agathon reminds me of a contemporary exchange. A distressed student told the Zen teacher Shunryu Suzuki that whenever he tried to meditate his mind was filled with strange and troubling thoughts. Suzuki replied: "Whatever bird flies through the sky, the sky doesn't care."[20] Our true nature is that vast empty spaciousness that nothing can stick to or defile. Painful thoughts arise, but, as the desert fathers stress, we are not our thoughts. It is not for sinful thoughts that we are condemned but only for making use of them.[21]

[19] *Sayings*, 23.

[20] *Zen Is Right Now: More Teaching Stories and Anecdotes of Shunryu Suzuki*, ed. David Chadwick (Boulder, CO: Shambhala, 2021), 6.

[21] See Merton, *Wisdom of the Desert*, 45.

Earlier we noted how the expression, "If you want to find rest" (then stop judging) implied the question: Do you truly seek rest? Most of us are somewhat attached to our restlessness and so make things harder for ourselves than they need to be. Nilus says: "The monk who loves interior peace will remain invulnerable to the shafts of the enemy, but he who mixes with crowds constantly receives blows."[22] While the peace that surpasses knowledge is a peace in the midst of conflict and not an escape, at the same time it's clear we deliberately undermine our peace of soul in countless ways.

Once we begin to cultivate stillness in earnest and have begun to taste that surpassing peace, we instinctively pull back from activity that would compromise it, as someone who's begun to exercise in earnest may gradually lose the taste for unhealthy food and behavior. Also, we are "invulnerable to the shafts of the enemy" when grounded in empathy and not judging. As we judge others so we will expect to be judged; if we're harsh with others we will live with the expectation of harsh judgment, however deeply suppressed. When we act from a place of genuine empathy, we are safe.

The modern Russian saint Seraphim of Sarov once said: "Keep your heart at peace and a multitude around you will be saved." Interior peace spills over into our everyday relationships so that our presence supports those around us in ways we're not even aware of; thus the importance of the quintessential monastic verse, "Keep your heart with all vigilance, / for from it flow the springs of life" (Prov 4:23). If we "love interior peace," we will keep watch over our thoughts, not to pounce on and suppress them but to allow them into the light and take care of the needs and energies they express.

[22] *Sayings*, 154.

Beyond Good and Evil

Carl Jung is famously supposed to have said, "I would rather be whole than good." There is a merely conventional "good" that isn't much better, and can even be worse, than "evil." Weil wrote: "Good as the opposite of evil is, in a sense, equivalent to it, as is the way with all opposites."[23] In effect Jung would rather be whole than good because he believes wholeness to be a greater good than the conventional "good" that is merely the opposite of evil. Better to bring all of ourselves as we are before the Lord like the publican than posture before him and make the case for our goodness like the Pharisee. Here is a story from the *Sayings*:

> A priest of Pelusia heard it said of some brethren that they often went to the city, took baths and were careless in their behavior. He went to the *synaxis*, and took the habit away from them. Afterwards, his heart was moved, he repented and went to see Abba Poemen, obsessed by his thoughts. He brought the monastic habits of the brothers and told him all about it. The old man said to him, "Don't you sometimes have something of the old Adam in you?" The priest said, "I have my share of the old Adam." The abba said to him, "Look, you are just like the brethren yourself; if you have even a little share of the old Adam, then you are subject to sin in the same way." So the priest went and called the brothers and asked their pardon; and he clothed them in the monastic habit again and let them go.[24]

The priest excludes the lax brothers from monastic life as he excludes from view the "old Adam" within himself. Poemen gently and adeptly puts his finger right on this, once again, like Jesus before those condemning the woman

[23] Weil, *Gravity and Grace*, 70.

[24] *Sayings*, 168.

caught in adultery. "You are just like the brethren yourself"; this likeness is what he's lost sight of. Not that he's behaved in the same way, but that he could easily be tempted and, without grace, just as easily fall. The radical embrace of limitation opens to boundless possibility, since "Anyone who is on good terms with his poverty is rich."[25]

The challenge is to bring all of ourselves before God. To fully defer to the judgment of God "who alone is good" and who is uniquely "light in which there is no darkness" we must renounce our own. Abba Poemen said, "To throw yourself before God, not to measure your progress, to leave behind all self-will; these are the instruments for the work of the soul."[26] These three are closely related. We throw all of ourselves before God, as we are, without judging and let go of the tendency to monitor our spiritual progress by some outside standard or expectation. Our transformation is ultimately God's work in us and proceeds in mysterious, sometimes baffling, ways. We have to trust that he wants us to grow and flourish more than we want it ourselves and knows far better how to bring it about, turning all things to good, to a good that is far more whole than the one we would construct left to ourselves.

So we must leave behind attachment to our own way, our expectations of who we should become and how we should bring it about. We grow more pliable and responsive to life. Frequently our experience is like that of the Israelites wandering aimlessly in the desert, following the cloud, breaking camp at a moment's notice to set out without

[25] Seneca, *Letters to Lucilius*, 4:11, in *The Epistle of Seneca*, vol. 1, trans. R. M. Gummere (New York: Putnam, 1934); quoted in William of Saint Thierry, *The Golden Epistle: A Letter to the Brethren at Mont Dieu*, trans. Theodore Berkeley, CF 12 (Collegeville, MN: Cistercian Publications, 1971), 43.

[26] *Sayings*, 172.

knowing where. In the experience of conversion we come away able to breathe more freely, sides of ourselves we had disavowed are brought to light and given play. The way to wholeness lies in entering fully into our absurdity and brokenness, fully owning the weak member we're so sorely tempted to lop off or at least ignore.

Poemen adds a twist to the counsel to not judge ourselves when he says, "Do not judge yourself but live with someone who knows how to behave himself properly."[27] We can learn more from living among wise people and seeing how they respond in complex situations than we can by following some abstract notion in our heads, especially since we tend to be alternately more indulgent and harsh with ourselves than we would be with another. A model (person, tradition, community) outside of and beyond the sphere of our own judgment can set us free from the tyranny of our own expectations.

"For," as Bernard writes, "who is so wretched a master, who so cruel a tyrant—one not at all sparing of the little slave subject to it—as a person's own will? Under her rule, one is never allowed to rest, never to relax! Like a cruel mistress—lacking all love and without mercy—she knows well how to exhaust you in her service. She drives you; she goads you on ever harder and burdens you ever more heavily."[28] Something in us would rather drive ourselves into the ground and retain the illusion of control than take on the "light burden and easy yoke" of Christ, obedience to another life within our own.

This has nothing to do with a facile and infantilized rejection of our freedom in order to avoid responsible life as an adult. We can use religion like that, to escape life, but

[27] *Sayings*, 177.

[28] Bernard of Clairvaux, "A Sermon for the Feast of St. Benedict," *Cistercian Studies Quarterly* 36, no. 3 (2001): 319.

the monastic path underlines the way our fears and fantasies actually short-circuit our attempts to be free. The popular sacralization of "autonomy," giving ourselves a law and a name, overlooks how quickly we're hijacked by passions that are not really our own at all, but alien to our true nature.

We need to apprentice ourselves to another to escape the tyranny of our own false self. This is another dimension of "I'd rather be whole than good." When we oppose one part of the self to another, whether in the direction of self-sacrifice or self-realization, at the root there is self reinforcing self, one part of the self acting on another, and so division. How can the self sacrifice the self? Or how can the self realize itself further? Perhaps this is part of the meaning of the great Japanese philosopher Dogen's statement, "To carry the self forward and experience myriad things is delusion. That myriad things come forth and experience themselves is awakening."[29]

"A brother said to Abba Poemen, 'If I fall into a shameful sin, my conscience devours and accuses me, saying, "Why have you fallen?"' The old man said to him, 'At the moment when a man goes astray, if he says, I have sinned, immediately the sin ceases.' "[30] And in another place, "Never worry about a thing once it's done."[31] This recalls the earlier discussion of true and false repentance. With false repentance we spin our wheels in futile self-recrimination where the repentance that comes from God carries with it bitter remorse but also a sense of possibility and even excitement about the way to make a change and begin to repair the damage.

[29] Dogen, *Moon in a Dewdrop: Writings of Zen Master Dogen*, trans. Kazuaki Tanahashi (New York: North Point Press, 1985), 69.

[30] *Sayings*, 181.

[31] See *Sayings*, 2.

Often we experience the grace of true repentance then doubt. We prefer our own judgment, however harsh, to another's, even God's. While sacramental confession is invaluable, a part of our need for the encouragement from and accountability to the wider community, it's important to recall that in the moment we repent from the heart we're forgiven. In a sense, we have to experience forgiveness in order to repent, in order to see our sin as sin. Letting go of our judgment is central to letting go of our (false) self, the self that is built up over and against another part of our self, that tries to reinforce and identify with one part by disavowing and excluding another, as the priest from Pelusia did when he lost touch with his own "share of the old Adam."

"When you include everything, that is the real self."[32] The self that includes everything is no self, no self we conceive of from outside. As with "God" we have a conceptual understanding of what is meant but the reality infinitely transcends our human ideas. Just as God is a spiritual and personal reality, not a conceptual one, so the human being "in the image of God" transcends our ideas. The mystery of a total human life transcends anything we say or think about it. In both cases there's the danger of a certain conceptual idolatry where we reduce a mysterious life to the clumsy categories of our limited thinking. The self that includes every facet and possibility of self is before thought, already there, a kind of zero-point, the free play of neutral between gears. In common experience, the times we are most fully alive we are forgetful of self; but when we are most constricted we feel self-conscious. In the space in which we are most ourselves we are wide open to "every-

[32] Shunryu Suzuki, *Not Always So: Practicing the True Spirit of Zen* (New York: HarperCollins, 2003), 114.

thing," including, allowing, accepting all because we are completely embraced, top to bottom, inside-out, immersed in the unconditional love of God.

One very common form of judging ourselves is by comparison with others, something the fathers frequently warn against. "Abba Poemen said that a brother who lived with some other brothers asked Abba Bessarion, 'What ought I to do?' The old man said to him, 'Keep silence and do not always be comparing yourself to others.' "[33] As in the story where one monk gives conferences all day but never breaks silence, while another who keeps exterior silence is said to have broken silence because he judges his brother in his heart, so here "silence" consists in not judging. Similarly, Poemen also said, "If you are silent, you will have peace wherever you live."[34] Such interior silence does not mean suppressing or piously pretending not to have any judgmental thoughts but allowing and making room for such thoughts without identifying with or acting on them. It means getting close to these painful thoughts and feelings and exploring what's behind them precisely without judging them. If we judge ourselves in advance for judgmental thoughts we'll never get to their root.

At the retreat house of our monastery we used to have a sign near the guestmaster's office, a saying from the fathers, "There is no trial whatsoever that comes to you that cannot be overcome by silence."[35] Eventually it was taken down, perhaps because it could give the impression that people ought to "tough it out" rather than share what was troubling them with another. As we've seen this would not be the approach of the fathers, who recognized how the

[33] *Sayings*, 178.
[34] *Sayings*, 178.
[35] See *Sayings*, 172.

enemy loved to deceive brothers into not sharing their thoughts out of shame or fear. In the current social context it could also carry the sense of not speaking up about injustice or misconduct in the church. The saying points instead, I believe, to the peace that surpasses understanding, a peace in the midst of, not apart from, conflict and distress, a peace and equanimity that is our true nature as persons in the image of the God of peace, the God whose bottomless tranquility is at all times and in every place the deepest reality. To live from such "silence" means we will have peace "wherever we live," and it will not be contingent on external circumstances. We choose a posture of not judging in whatever context and receive peace in return.

"Some old men came to see Abba Poemen and said to him, 'When we see brothers who are dozing at the *synaxis*, shall we rouse them so that they will be watchful?' He said to them, 'For my part when I see a brother who is dozing, I put his head on my knees and let him rest.' "[36] To wake the brother would not only deprive him of sleep he clearly needs but subject him to shame, or at least embarrassment. Change induced by fear, shame, and judging is short-lived at best. Only the experience of gratuitous love can provoke a free, equally gratuitous and lasting effort, can inspire a person to change from within. Asleep during liturgy the brother is exposed and vulnerable. If he wakes to find that he's not only been allowed to sleep but treated with respect and even tenderness he may be moved to greater fervor and vigilance, assured of fraternal support.

As in scripture (Rom 12:20)—"if your enemies are hungry, feed them; if they are thirsty, give them something to drink, for by doing this you will heap burning coals on their heads"—here, in a much gentler register the same logic

[36] *Sayings*, 92.

applies. Falling asleep in choir is a fairly minor infraction, a symptom of human weakness more than a moral flaw. But even in cases where we are accused and attacked unjustly, we're challenged to "overcome evil with good" and not react in kind. When Jesus says, "Do not resist an evildoer" (Matt 5:39), I think he means never fight evil with evil or respond to passion with passion. The gospel clearly demands that we interrupt this deeply ingrained mimetic tendency and love and forgive on the model of Jesus, rather than that of our aggressor.

Jesus is not only or mainly an external model for us but he lives and moves within and through us by his Spirit; as in Romans (12:2): "Do not be conformed to this age, but be transformed by the renewing of the mind, so that you may discern what is the will of God—what is good and acceptable and perfect." The standard of the world divides one part over and against another where the standard of the Christian is Christ crucified, the sign of contradiction who, when lifted up, draws all things to himself (John 12:32).

In the early church, monks were seen as mourners, those who lament for and grieve over the terrible injustice and suffering in human life. This is brought out powerfully in the following account: "Abba Joseph related that Abba Isaac said, 'I was sitting with Abba Poemen one day and I saw him in ecstasy and [as] I was on terms of great freedom of speech with him, I prostrated myself before him and begged him, saying, "Tell me where you were." He was forced to answer and he said, "My thought was with Saint Mary, the Mother of God, as she wept by the cross of the Saviour. I wish I could always weep like that."'"[37]

[37] *Sayings*, 187.

Instead of our own standard or that of the world, the one true judgment is the cross. There Jesus exposed both our original innocence, the manner in which we came into the world helpless and suffered without in any way deserving to, and the nature of sin: how we scapegoat and exclude the other. We also exclude what we find shameful or frightening in ourselves so that in a certain sense self-hatred can be seen at the root of "original sin." Jesus on the cross reveals the tragedy of our original innocence and the ways we've brutally punished it in ourselves and others.

As "No one lights a lamp and puts it under a basket," Christ is raised onto the lampstand of the cross as a sign of contradiction to bring to light the thoughts of many hearts. In the same moment in which the full truth of our callousness and cruelty is exposed he reveals the boundless, gratuitous love of God. Poemen wants to weep as Mary did. How was that? She wept over her only child: "When they look on the one whom they have pierced, they shall mourn for him, as one mourns for an only child and weep bitterly over him as one weeps over a firstborn" (Zech 12:10). She saw with piercing clarity the goodness of Jesus and the ruthless stupidity with which human beings spat in his face—and in the same moment, the moment of unbearable anguish and bitter grief was pervaded by the bottomless tranquility of God. Sharing her sorrow is the way beyond all violence and division.

CHAPTER THREE

Acceptance

The Brothers Karamazov

What might happen if a desert father were time-warped into modernity? How might he guide someone called to be a monk in "the world"? In his masterwork, *The Brothers Karamazov*, Dostoevsky prophetically depicts a particular expression of the desert path of not judging as the antidote to the murderous rivalry and isolation consuming the modern world.[1] His "elder Zosima" teaches that we are each fundamentally guilty (or "responsible") to all for everything, and to realize this, to take it all on oneself freely is paradise. Only Jesus, who "became sin," has taken the place of one guilty to all for everything, so perhaps part of what the elder has in view is precisely a kind of union with Jesus in taking on the sin and suffering of others.[2]

At a certain point in the story the proud, intellectual Ivan abruptly cuts ties with his family and sets off alone for Moscow. Instead of taking on another's sin, he passes his

[1] Fyodor Dostoevsky, *The Brothers Karamazov: A Novel in Four Parts with Epilogue*, trans. Richard Pevear and Larissa Volokhonsky (New York: Farrar, Straus and Giroux, 1990).

[2] Needless to say, there are unhelpful or distorted ways of taking responsibility for other people's flaws.

desire to murder his father on to his half-brother, who carries out Ivan's unspoken wish. Alyosha, the book's hero, by contrast, is sent away from the monastery by his elder and by obedience plunged into the tortuous entanglements of his brothers and friends. Instead of Ivan's clean break, the modernist dream of autonomy, he sets to work as a peacemaker in the midst of rivalrous conflicts that nearly devour him. He actively takes responsibility for the failings of his brothers and their complex implications. At times scorned as naïve, but also loved, trusted, and accorded a certain respect for his sincerity, Alyosha shows what it means to be a brother. "Until one has indeed become the brother of all, there will be no brotherhood."[3] In Dostoevsky's vision, we become the brother of all by taking the lowest place, the place of the scapegoat. We take the blame on ourselves and seek pardon.

The Brothers Karamazov can be read as a kind of extended parody-meditation on the parable of the prodigal son. This is suggested, for instance, by the early chapter heading, "The First Son Sent Packing." Instead of the younger son being entrusted with his complete inheritance even before the death of the father, the older son (Dimitri) is "sent packing" by his stingy, lascivious father, Fyodor, having been deceived and shortchanged of the money due him. Here Dimitri is akin to the reckless, hedonistic prodigal and the next son Ivan, with his lofty moral indignation, the son who stays at home. The elder Zosima models the true father. He contains in himself the vitality of Dimitri and the moral passion of Ivan but in a spiritual and integrated form. The youngest brother, Alyosha, Zosima's spiritual heir, is challenged over the course of the book to

[3] Dostoevsky, *Brothers Karamazov*, 303.

himself become a "father" like Zosima and to reconcile his two brothers, both in fact and within himself.

Before launching into his famous poem of the Grand Inquisitor, Ivan details a disturbing array of "true crime" accounts of children suffering ghastly torture. He concludes with the decision to "return his ticket" to a universe in which the good of the many is built upon the destruction of the innocent. Though marked by a certain proud indignation and a love that is more abstract than concrete—like several other characters in the book he loves humanity but strains to love particular human beings—the account so far attests genuine compassion and concern for victims, a just outrage at human cruelty.

But Ivan blames God and the metaphysical rather than human order for such violence. The "solution" he proposes in the legend of the Grand Inquisitor works precisely by the exclusion and replacement of the innocent Christ and the freedom to which he calls human beings. The Inquisitor represents at some level the emerging elite of secular revolutionary social engineers. The terrible violence against the innocent is the result of human, not divine violence, and the gesture of "returning the ticket" simply masks the disowning and cloaking of responsibility. In this respect it is the antithesis of Zosima's ideal of the willingness to be "guilty to all for everything," to stand in the place of the persecuted and excluded and to suffer with them.

Very broadly, it's not hard to see both dimensions of this outlook in various secular ideologies today: a genuine, sometimes heroic, concern for victims, one that is often far ahead of the church in decrying injustice and standing with the marginal, and a despotic social engineering eager to lift from humanity's shoulders the heavy burden of authentic freedom. The state positions itself as sole protector of individual freedom ("rights") over against mediating communities like families, unions, churches, which it portrays as backward and controlling. Of course by systematically weakening such institutions and moving individuals to rely more and more on the state alone, the effective freedom of individuals is subtly, gradually, diminished.

In their attitude toward "the world" Christians replicate the division: some stress the genuine concern for victims among secular movements and emphasize the ways they are more Christian than the church in their prophetic solidarity with those on the margins; while others focus exclusively on the despotic, social engineering maneuvers of secular political elites, unwilling to admit even a grain of real concern for victims. The first tend to replace anything recognizably Christian with social commitments, while the second fail to heed, and often react defensively against, the valuable challenge and critique offered by many secular movements where "seeds of the Word" are clearly germinating.

Alyosha's response to Ivan's magnificent, feverish diatribe is twofold. Immediately, and to Ivan's delight, Alyosha kisses him on the lips, as Christ does the Grand Inquisitor in the legend. Part of the sense of this mysterious and provocative sign would seem to be that Alyosha validates the goodness present in Ivan and his real concern for victims, as Christ does, even for the Grand Inquisitor. At numerous points in the story Alyosha embodies the willingness of God to accept even the most meager good deed and to forgive enormous sins in return, as in Grushenka's folktale of the onion given by a sinner to a poor woman.

Next, Alyosha spends the rest of the book putting into practice the way of active love advocated by the elder Zosima. He serves as a peacemaker and voice of conscience that brings out the best in others, even his father Fyodor, precisely by his refusal to judge them. In obedience to Zosima, he becomes a "monk in the world" demonstrating what it means to take on himself the guilt of others. Alyosha willingly becomes entangled in the concrete particulars, the pettiness and banality of real people, and works to alleviate their misery. Ivan by contrast, as we have seen, breaks all ties with his family at the critical moment, paving the way for the murder of his father which he secretly desires. So with spontaneous admiration, without any trace of condescension, Alyosha first honors the nobility of Ivan's soul as revealed in his passionate concern for innocent victims of cruelty. Then he refutes the social engineering inquisition not by posturing, not with a competing storyline, but by the witness of a gentle but relentless active love. This twofold approach seems to me to be a promising, intensely challenging, way forward for Christians today.

Both the church of the Grand Inquisitor and the state that vies to replace it are completely paternalistic. The desert father tradition represented by Zosima offers the alternative of a fatherhood lived as brotherhood. In the truly Christian community there are no fathers, only brothers and sisters. "Call no one on earth father, master, teacher, for you are all brothers" (see Matt 23:8-9). It is possible Jesus established men as priests precisely to counter and undermine patriarchy. Precisely by dressing the paterfamilias in elaborate robes only to (sacramentally) feed, clothe, and bathe the people, performing the work of female slaves, the idolatry of the patriarch is exposed and ironized. Popes and bishops dressed in royal purple began to compete in earnest with the kings and emperors they were meant to parody and the church went, at times terribly, off-track, for want of *irony*.

The desert tradition is present in *The Brothers Karamazov* not only in the figure of Zosima but in the mysterious presence of a book of sayings by Isaac of Syria, a seventh-century desert monk and mystic. The book appears a few times at strategic points in the narrative, including in the hands of the murderer Smerdyakov—it's on his table when Ivan last encounters him—suggesting perhaps that even the most

Alice Neel. *Illustrations to The Brothers Karamazov by Fyodor Dostoyevsky. Untitled (Karamazov, His Three Sons and the Servant Gregory)*, c. 1938. Ink on paper. Paper: 14 1/4 x 10 inches. 36.2 x 25.4 cm. © The Estate of Alice Neel. Courtesy The Estate of Alice Neel and David Zwirner.

vile are not excluded by the way of mercy. Not only the book but the text makes a covert appearance at a key moment in one of Zosima's speeches adapted from a text by Isaac. The desert focus on mercy and not judging receives a particular emphasis in the work of Isaac of Syria, as we'll see in a future chapter devoted to his writings.

There are a number of stories from the desert in which monks choose to take a brother's sins on themselves. In one, two monks go into town on business. They separate for a time and when they join up again one has fallen into sexual sin. Deeply troubled and ashamed, he feels he can't return to the monastery. His brother persuades him to return by promising to say they both fell into sin and sharing his penance—and this is what happens. After a few days an angel reveals to one of the elders that God has forgiven the sin of the one brother for the sake of the other's mercy.

In another story brothers have convened to exclude a monk who has fallen into sin. Abba Pior, who keeps quiet at the meeting, is later seen walking about with two leaky sand bags, a large one behind him, a small one in front. When asked about the meaning of this performance he says, "In this sack which contains much sand, are my sins, which are many; I have put them behind me so as not to be troubled by them and so as not to weep; and see here are the sins of my brother which are right in front of me and I spend my time judging them. This is not right. I ought rather to carry my sins in front of me and concern myself with them, begging God to forgive me for them." The others are struck to the heart and declare, "Truly, this is the way to salvation."[4]

[4] *The Sayings of the Desert Fathers: The Alphabetical Collection*, trans. Benedicta Ward, CS 59 (Collegeville, MN: Cistercian Publications, 1984), 199–200.

Clear awareness of how constantly the passions leak into our thoughts and skew our actions would keep us from fixating on the faults of others. Even if we have not actively fallen into actual sin, we know and see clearly how the seeds of every sin lie buried within us; we are humbled, and refrain from judging. A similar story is told of Abba Moses. In Scetis, brothers convened a council to consider the case of a brother who had fallen. Moses refused to attend. When summoned, he appeared trailing water from a leaky jug and when asked about the sign declared, "My sins run out behind me and I do not see them, and today I am coming to judge the errors of another."[5] Constantly holding in mind that we're never seeing the whole story and always inclined to mask and minimize our own faults engenders a disposition of humble mercy to all.

Overacceptance

The dramatic gestures of the fathers in stories like these recall the prophetic signs performed by first testament prophets. They expose and amplify the dynamics in play at the critical point where a community tips over into condemnation. The abbas take the place of the brother under judgment and reflect back to the judges the nature of their own sin. They don't make speeches on behalf of the persecuted but acknowledge and dramatize their sins (sand, water) so the community can see their own.

Earlier we touched on Samuel Wells's discussion of "overacceptance," in which instead of simply rejecting or going along with a dramatic "offer," the actor embraces it completely and spins it in some creative new direction. Wells gives numerous instances of Jesus overaccepting dif-

[5] *Sayings*, 138–39.

ferent situations in the gospels. Memorably, he also relates the story of a pianist about to perform before a packed concert hall, when a young girl breaks from her mortified parents, leaps onto the stage, and begins to pound away at the keys in wild cacophony. The pianist retains his composure, listens a moment, then steps up behind the girl and, placing one hand on either side of hers, begins to improvise a melody around bits and traces picked out from her play.[6]

It is in just this way that God relates to our sins and in this spirit the desert fathers act as they do. In other words they make themselves guilty to all for everything and take on their brothers' sins, in full creative freedom not self-flagellation. Jesus' embrace of the cross—his orchestration of the trial, his prophetic framing of his death in the eucharist—is the supreme moment of such overacceptance. Like any good improv artist, he didn't know exactly how the play would turn out but threw himself into unfolding events with reckless abandon and confident trust.

Abba Paphnutius rarely drank wine. Once, accosted by robbers who knew this, he was told he must drink the cup of wine offered him or be killed. He drank readily but the leader of the band was mortified and promised never again to harm anyone. "So the old man converted the whole band by giving up his own will for the Lord's sake."[7] He wasn't afraid to be martyred but didn't want the robbers to incur the guilt of killing him. He drinks, we read, "knowing that he was fulfilling the commandment of God and in order to win the confidence of the robber." He readily puts aside attachment to his own ascetic program for the sake of a greater good.

[6] Samuel Wells, *Improvisation: The Drama of Christian Ethics* (Grand Rapids, MI: Brazos, 2004), 131–32.

[7] *Sayings*, 202.

The saying of Paphnutius directly after this reveals his secret: "Wherever you go, do not judge yourself and you will be at peace."[8] A monk whose sense of himself was inseparable from his particular ascetic regime might have insisted on not drinking, even dying as a kind of martyr, with no thought for the will of God; never mind what might be best for the robbers. Paphnutius feels his way into his response only because he is willing to roll with and be guided by events. His first reaction is not to block and insist on his scripted lines, but overaccept and unite with the Spirit in "turning all to good."

Such an approach springs from and further cultivates liberty of spirit. "When Abba Romanus was at the point of death, his disciples gathered around him and said, 'How ought we to conduct ourselves?' The old man said to them, 'I do not think I have ever told one of you to do something, without having first made the decision not to get angry, if what I said were not done; and so we have lived in peace all our days.'"[9] Romanus lives in readiness to roll forward and not react in kind when confronted with a block, and his flexibility spills over into peace for the whole community.

"Do Not Judge Yourself"

I'd like to tease out a little further here this saying of Paphnutius: "Wherever you go, do not judge yourself and you will be at peace."[10] Not to judge ourselves includes not judging ourselves to be innocent: it's not exoneration or permissiveness. Rather we defer all judgment to God. As St. Paul says, "I do not even judge myself. I am not aware of anything against myself but I am not thereby acquitted"

[8] *Sayings*, 202.
[9] *Sayings*, 211.
[10] *Sayings*, 203.

(1 Cor 4:3-4). We own and take responsibility for our conduct but leave aside all comparison and measurement. God alone knows our full context and can alone adjudicate guilt and innocence rightly. To judge our actions is one thing but Paphnutius speaks of judging ourselves. We may behave poorly, for whatever combination of reasons and with whatever degree of culpability, but we remain indelibly "in the image of God," however disfigured.

Bernard declared that no matter what a person had done he could not only hope for pardon but eventual union with God.[11] "Judging," as we've been coming to understand it, is obsessive, reactive, and divisive. When we judge ourselves we pit one part of ourselves against another and succeed only in pushing what we disown (dark or light) further into shadow. As we read previously, "When you include everything, that is the real self" (Suzuki). The true self already includes and allows everything. It's a kind of clearing or zero point, allowing all to arise and fall away, without judging. It takes responsibility for all, takes care of all. It's this self and this disposition that is cultivated by contemplative prayer, by prayer beyond words or images comprised of presence, trust, and surrender.[12]

That judgment of others alienates us from ourselves is indicated in the following story by Abba Isaac's inability to reenter his cell:

> One day Abba Isaac went to a monastery. He saw a brother committing a sin and he condemned him. When he returned to the desert, an angel of the Lord came and stood in front

[11] Bernard of Clairvaux, *On the Song of Songs IV*, trans. Irene Edmonds, CF 40 (Collegeville, MN: Liturgical Press, 1980), 189.

[12] Hal and Sidra Stone, *Embracing Your Inner Critic: Turning Self-Criticism into a Creative Asset* (San Francisco: HarperSanFrancisco, 1993), 161: "The best way to avoid being judged by others is not to judge yourself."

> of the door of his cell, and said, "I will not let you enter." But he persisted, saying, "What is the matter?" and the angel replied, "God has sent me to ask you where you want to throw the guilty brother whom you have condemned." Immediately he repented and said, "I have sinned, forgive me." Then the angel said, "Get up, God has forgiven you. But from now on, be careful not to judge someone before God has done so."[13]

Presuming to take the place of God we fall away from our own ground, are cut off from where we actually stand. The sense of dislocation can point up to us when we've fallen out of tune. God here "overaccepts" Isaac's presumption to take his place as judge by sending his angel to ask what he's supposed to do with this sinner—heaven or hell? The shocking gravity of such a decision makes Isaac realize his sin right away. How could he possibly know the whole story of this person he so casually presumed to judge? The angel's statement prompts Isaac to see the one he's judged not as the sum of his worst behavior but as a person made by God and destined for eternal life.

The deferral of judgment to God alone requires allowing the weeds and wheat to grow together, and taking fish of every kind into the net. God will "judge" in his own time and way but what that will look like we're unable to say. We know that he wills the salvation of all and that his thoughts and ways are not our own. With regards to leaving judgment to God alone, Paul writes: "Beloved, never avenge yourselves, but leave room for the wrath of God, for it is written, 'Vengeance is mine; I will repay, says the Lord.' Instead, 'if your enemies are hungry, feed them; if they are thirsty, give them something to drink, for by doing this you will heap burning coals on their heads'" (Rom 12:19-20).

[13] *Sayings*, 109–10.

This of course raises the question of what wrath and vengeance might look like to an all-merciful God. They might look like the gratuitous mercy he enjoins, feeding one's enemies to "heap burning coals" of compunction on their heads and spark a free response of repentance, "for he himself is kind to the ungrateful and the wicked" (Luke 6:35). Otherwise: does God hold himself to a lower standard than he holds us? Surely "vengeance" can't have the sense here of simply rebounding mimetically off the other's violence. We are to become "children of our heavenly Father" and perfect as he is by doing good to all and overcoming evil with good, "for he makes his rain fall and sun shine on good and bad alike" (see Matt 5:43-45). The stance of not judging involves a kind of "non-dual" horizon where contraries are allowed to coexist without any forced or premature attempt at resolution.

Revenge

In one of the sayings a brother comes to Abba Sisoes wanting to avenge himself on a brother who had wronged him. When the old man pleads with him to relent, he is told, "I shall not rest until I have avenged myself." At this point the Abba invites him to pray and begins, "'God, we no longer need you to care for us, since we do justice for ourselves.' Hearing these words, the brother fell at the old man's feet, saying, 'I will no longer seek justice from my brother; forgive me, abba.'"[14] Sisoes locates justice within God's providential "care" for his creatures and so presents our taking justice into our own hands as a failure to trust in that providence. If we give up allowing God alone to judge, we also give up reliance on his unfailing care. If sin

[14] *Sayings*, 212.

is its own worst punishment and it is the nature of evil to recoil on itself, then we have only to step out of the way and pay attention, perhaps even seeking to soften the blow for those locked in sin. Again, not judging does not mean permissiveness, which is a lack of care, or even tolerance, but withdrawal from action, not repaying evil for evil, not resisting an evildoer, so as not to become entangled in their contagious rage.

"A brother questioned Abba Hierax saying, 'Give me a word. How can I be saved?' The old man said to him, 'Sit in your cell, and if you are hungry, eat, if you are thirsty, drink; only do not speak evil of anyone, and you will be saved.' "[15] Here, refraining from judgment in the form of running others down is ranked higher than every ascetic practice. One can eat and drink as they like so long as they don't speak evil of others. Fasting and the other practices are seen by implication as a means to the end of not judging. Because we won't be able to withhold judgment, we can't eat and drink with abandon but need hunger and thirst to remind us of our poverty and the need to show mercy. One who refrains from speaking evil of others brings salvation insofar as he demonstrates a life transformed by grace, showing to others the mercy he has received.

The Accuser loves nothing more than to turn human beings against one another. The "remembrance of God" is tied closely to the awareness that we are all on the same side fighting against the passions. "Abba Macarius said, 'If we remember the wrongs which men have done us, we destroy the power of the remembrance of God. But if we remind ourselves of the evil deeds of the demons, we shall be invulnerable.' "[16] Rather than "demonize" our fellow human

[15] *Sayings*, 104.
[16] *Sayings*, 136.

beings, recalling evil in a less distilled form can clarify and bring perspective to our situation. God is God, demons are demons, human beings are neither. Resentment and the desire for vengeance occlude awareness of God in part because we tend to imagine God in the image of our own inner state.

The last word in this discussion of the *Sayings* goes to Abba Moses. In a somewhat shocking exchange, he is asked what a slave ought to say when beaten for a fault and replies that he ought simply to say, "Forgive me, I have sinned." Even his contemporary interlocutor seems a bit amazed by this and asks, "Nothing else?" "The old man said, 'No, for from the moment he takes upon himself responsibility for the affair and says, "I have sinned," immediately the Lord will have mercy on him. The aim in all these things is not to judge one's neighbour.' "[17] Someone in an unjust position of subjection suffering excessive, violent punishment for doing wrong is enjoined to "overaccept" not only his own limited guilt but willingly undergo its excessive punishment. Sayings like this ought to carry a "Do not try this at home" warning, and we recall that the intended audience was other monks in the desert, experienced practitioners who had renounced everything to find liberty of spirit.

The *Sayings* are not universal prescriptions applicable everywhere for all people but particular words given to particular brothers at a given moment on their path based on the spiritual discernment of the elder speaking. Moses himself was not opposed to defending himself. A former highway robber feared throughout the land, he was once set upon by robbers after his conversion. He overpowered his attackers, tied them up in a great bundle and laid them at the feet of the elders asking what he was to do with them.

[17] *Sayings*, 142.

(As usual in these stories they all repent and become his disciples!)

In the case of the slave beaten unjustly, part of the teaching may be that while we can't change the conduct of others we can take responsibility for our own fault, even if that appears quite small by comparison. Better to do the possible than try to change another by coercion. By taking responsibility for his fault, the "slave" (standing in for the desert monk) resists the temptation to react in kind, by counterattacking his master for treating him abusively. Moses speaks of the slave "taking responsibility for the affair" which suggests perhaps the "whole" affair, even his master's overreaction, in a way akin to what the elder Zosima envisioned: "be guilty to all for all," stand in the place of the unrighteous and take blame on yourself without discriminating, rather than blaming others.

This raises again the question of how this could possibly apply in cases of systemic injustice like racial prejudice or gender disparity where often the persecuted holds a highly negative view of themselves in the wake of years (centuries) of abusive treatment. The judgment of the persecutor has been deeply internalized such that victims are judging themselves. "Not judging" in such a case means dissolving one's internalization of another's harsh judgment. To complacently accept the beating would be, in Wells terms, simply to "accept" the (unjust) terms of the role-play inherited.

Moses is imagining something more like an "overacceptance" of blame that in a kind of nonviolent resistance steps beyond the circle of mimetic reactivity and spins the drama in a fresh direction, offering the other a new opening, a way out of the abusive cycle, where to react with counter-blame and anger would only reinforce it. Needless to say, the issues are complex and much more could be said. I just want to indicate a direction here in which sayings like this can be interpreted. Moses himself extrapolates on the sense he intends, and his words are worth citing at length:

> To die to one's neighbour is this: To bear your own faults and not to pay attention to anyone else wondering whether they are good or bad. Do no harm to anyone, do not think anything bad in your heart towards anyone, do not scorn the man who does evil, do not put confidence in him who does wrong to his neighbour, do not rejoice with him who injures his neighbour. This is what dying to one's neighbour means. Do not rail against anyone, but rather say, "God knows each one." Do not agree with him who slanders, do not rejoice at his slander and do not hate him who slanders his neighbour. This is what it means not to judge.[18]

The striking expression "dying to one's neighbour" suggests non-reactivity, not getting hooked into another's programming. As so often in the *Sayings*, the challenge is to redirect our attention away from the faults of others and back to our own, and this in a spirit of humility and compunction, not outrage. We are not surprised or scandalized by our sin but entrust ourselves to divine mercy simply and with confidence.

As Bernard teaches, the saint is not one who never falls, but one who gets up quickly after a fall and keeps going, lifting his eyes from his own *miseria* to God's *misericordia*. Doing no harm extends to the interior, as in Jesus' teaching where intentional lust and anger in the heart mean one has already fallen. Not judging doesn't mean we accept or collude with the other's conduct, or despise him for it, knowing we too are prone to the same. Judgment is deferred: "God knows each one." Moses concludes, "Do not have hostile feelings towards anyone and do not let dislike dominate

[18] *Sayings*, 142–43.

your heart; do not hate him who hates his neighbour. This is what peace is: Encourage yourself with this thought, 'Affliction lasts but a short time, while peace is for ever, by the grace of God the Word. Amen.'"[19] Not denying our hostile feelings the challenge is rather not to be controlled by them. The goal is to retain genuine liberty of spirit. Encouragement comes with the twofold recognition of the radical transience of life on earth and its attendant suffering, while the "peace that surpasses understanding," the eternal serenity of the divine is already and forever the deepest ground of all reality, suffusing and pervading each moment.

[19] *Sayings*, 143.

CHAPTER FOUR

Compassion

On Refusal to Judge Our Neighbor

The sixth-century saint Dorotheos is one of the more personable and humane figures to emerge from the desert tradition. His writings crystallize and refine that tradition in a distinctive way and one has the sense of someone speaking from experience, a real personality shining through the lines. His discourse "On Refusal to Judge Our Neighbor" takes up and creatively develops numerous threads we've touched on, commenting in places on several of the stories and sayings we've explored.

As we might expect, Dorotheos begins by highlighting the disparity between the attention we give the sins of others and the blindness we have to our own. "Because we become careless about our own faults and do not lament our own death (as the Fathers put it), we lose the power to correct ourselves and we are always at work on our neighbor. Nothing angers God so much or strips a man so bare or carries him off so effectively to his ruin as calumniating, condemning or despising his neighbor." Lack of concern over our faults coincides with ignoring, instead of embracing and working within, limitation, ultimately the limitation of death. We lose "the power to correct ourselves" because we can only change effectively if we start from where we actually are, with a humble recognition of our poverty and the transient nature of life. We begin to see why the desert fathers focused so keenly on not judging others: judgment saps our power to change, angers God more than any other sin, and is "very nearly the most difficult of all sins to deal with."[1]

Dorotheos specifies three elements or degrees in judging that progress in gravity. We run a person down when we report their poor behavior to others, condemn when we say that because they acted poorly they are horrible people. Lastly, we despise another for their sin. Dorotheos underlines the difference between reporting that a person grew angry and stating that he is an angry person: "This is a very serious thing. For it is one thing to say, 'He got mad,' and another thing to say, 'He is bad-tempered,' and to reveal, as we said, the whole disposition of his life. It is serious to judge a man for each one of his sins. As Christ himself says, 'Hypocrite, first take the board from your own eye, then you can see to take the splinter out of your brother's eye.'" In the very next line Dorotheos identifies the "board" with our "rash judgment," a greater sin and one that blinds far more than whatever speck we imagine in our brother's eye.

Losing sight of our limits and faults, we fail to see how the passions skew our vision. Judging others harshly for what we overlook in ourselves creates the board in our eye that blinds us. The other's fault appears so enormous because the obstruction is so close to us, lodged in our own eye. "Why are we so ready to judge our neighbor? Why are we so concerned about the burden of others?"[2] We are obsessed with that burden because it belongs to us. We tie up

[1] Dorotheos of Gaza, *Discourses and Sayings*, trans. Eric P. Wheeler, CS 33 (Collegeville, MN: Cistercian Publications, 1977), 131–32.

[2] Dorotheos, *Discourses*, 132–33.

the heavy burden of our disavowed weakness for others to carry without lifting a finger to help.

Dorotheos glosses the story of the Pharisee and the publican, explaining that the Pharisee was not condemned for giving thanks to God for his good works—he was telling the truth!—and not for saying "I am not like others" but only for saying "I am not like this tax-collector." "It was then that he made a judgment. He condemned a person and the dispositions of his soul—to put it shortly, his whole life."[3] The Pharisee imagines he can read the soul of the publican and reduces him to his worst behavior. Much of what we take to be "personality" is in fact conditioning. The passions dehumanize and depersonalize, obscuring our true nature. So to identify the person with the conduct that keeps him stuck is an act at once of presumption and despair. We presume to read minds and despair of the other's intrinsic goodness and power to change. The same applies when we judge ourselves reductively as the sum total of the ways we've been hurt and our faltering attempts to medicate the pain.

That the reduction of the other to their worst behavior actually prevents them from changing is stated strikingly by a modern "desert father," Charles de Foucauld: "From the moment in which we begin to judge anyone, to limit our confidence in him, from the moment at which we identify the person with what we know of him and so reduce him to that, we cease to love the person and he ceases to be able to become better. We should expect everything of everyone. We must dare to be love in a world that does not know how to love."[4] Here "to judge" means to limit our trust in the intrinsic goodness and dignity of the other person

[3] Dorotheos, *Discourses*, 132.

[4] Joseph Diele, *Jesus Day by Day with Blessed Charles de Foucauld and His Family* (Fort Mill, SC: Jesus Caritas Publications, 2018), 39.

and instead to reduce them to what "we know," that is, their problematic behavior. Withholding love then, also means withholding faith in the other's ineradicable being in the image of God and hope of their growing into its likeness. Strikingly, Charles de Foucauld holds that by judging the other we effectively prevent their conversion. If this seems too strong we need only consider how love and encouragement form the necessary environment for growth to see how withholding them prevents it.

Dorotheos asks why we don't judge our own faults, since they are the ones for which we have unique "inside" knowledge, and the ones for which we are accountable before God. If we "judge" ourselves humbly, realistically, judgment in the sense of condemnation is turned to discretion, the spiritual discrimination that can see how our conditioning is at work within us. We gain some distance from the storylines by which we tend to be hypnotized. Judging ourselves in the sense of reducing ourselves to our worst behavior is no more accurate or helpful with ourselves than it is with others. If we can see our own complexity simply and with empathy we'll be able to extend the same generous perspective to others. And vice versa. It sometimes happens that we need to accept something within us before we can accept it in another. But it also seems to play out that by struggling to get along with another person we come to accept an aspect of ourselves we couldn't have come to terms with otherwise. This is a key dimension of life in community—whether family, parish, work, or a monastery.

Dorotheos underlines that it's not our place to judge others. They belong to God and we usurp divine prerogative when we presume to judge. Recalling Paul's, "Who are you to judge the slave of another?" he asks, "Why should we demand a reckoning from his creature, his servant?" He next comments on the story we touched on above concerning the monk who, after judging his brother, is confronted by an angel who announces that the brother has just died, and demands to know whether the brother is to be spared or punished. He relates that the old man was grieved over this to his dying day.[5]

Dorotheos stresses the complexity of human life and situations, the varied contexts in which sin occurs, arguing that only God can see the full story. "He knows the state of each one of us and our capacities, our deviations, and our gifts, our constitution and our preparedness, and it is for him to judge each of these things according to the knowledge that he alone has. . . . Who could understand all these judgments except the one who has done everything, formed everything and knows everything?"[6]

He gives the example of two young girls, sisters, separated from one another at a young age, one raised in ideal, the other in unfortunate conditions. If they both fall into the same sin, will they be judged equally? He goes on to point out that if we see someone fall, we don't see how hard they fought before falling or how sincerely they may have repented. He touches on the effect judgment has on the judge: "how are you going to sit in judgment and constrict your own soul?" and speaks of "ruining our own soul" by judging that of another.[7] To speak of judgment "constricting" the soul strikes me as especially apt. Judging others involves a narrowing, a stiffness, a reduction in our sense of possibility, where the way of non-judgment, by contrast, brings a *dilatatio cordis*, an expansion of heart, a letting go, a relaxation that includes a willingness to suffer and to suffer with others.

[5] Dorotheos, *Discourses*, 133.

[6] Dorotheos, *Discourses*, 133.

[7] Dorotheos, *Discourses*, 135.

At this point Dorotheos circles back to the third and most serious dimension of judging, when instead of commenting on another's fault or identifying the person with their poor behavior, we despise them because of it. With great acuity, he writes, "Contempt adds to condemnation the desire to set someone at nought—as if the neighbor were a bad smell which has to be got rid of as something disgusting, and this is worse than rash judgment and exceedingly destructive."[8] To get to the point where we want the other to be erased, to cease to exist, we must reduce them in our minds to a shell of themselves, a caricature, and overlook their reality as a unique and particular person. They have instead become a type, an avatar for something so despicable we can't bear for it to exist. The scorn we express of course inflates a sense of our own superiority.

In contrast, Dorotheos writes, "Those who want to be saved scrutinize not the shortcomings of their neighbor but always their own and they set about eliminating them."[9] Without exception ("always") they begin from a frank recognition of their own faults and they do so in such a way that they are empowered to make a change. They eliminate their faults instead of eliminating another person they've made to represent them. As we touched on earlier, the difference between true and false repentance is that where the latter simply spins its wheels in self-hatred, the grace of genuine conversion involves at once the awareness of our wretchedness and the impulse to make a change. We see how we've been wrong and are eager to work hard to repair the damage.

Dorotheos notes how blithely we poison others by despising our neighbor in their presence. In this we do the

[8] Dorotheos, *Discourses*, 135.

[9] Dorotheos, *Discourses*, 135.

work of the devil, the Accuser. "We are found to work with him for our own destruction and that of our neighbor, for a man who harms his own soul is working with, and helping, the devil. The man who seeks to profit his soul is cooperating with the angels."[10] Scorn, especially with a moralistic cast, is highly contagious, but by accusing others we harm ourselves. By building them up, we are healed.

Regarding scorn, Buddhist tradition speaks of a bodhisattva whose name means "Never-Despising-Anyone." He went about bowing with great respect before everyone he encountered, convinced that each one would soon awaken and realize their true nature. He was often mocked and ridiculed for his practice. For someone to express respect for all and on the basis of their inherent worth rather than any conventional human marker can be deeply subversive, showing up our attachment to the status quo and its injustices.

Shared scorn often becomes the toxic glue between potential rivals, as when Pilate and Herod, who were enemies, "become friends" on the day they ally against Jesus. When we're speaking with someone who puts us on edge it's very tempting to find a common target and forge a superficial peace on the basis of this shared animus. Of course this only reinforces the mind of "judging," the "world's" divisive way of thinking, on which no true peace can be established.

Humble respect for the dignity of every human life, made in the image of God, destined for deification, powerfully undermines the tendency to judge. It must be deliberately cultivated and expressed to reverse the effects of toxic rivalry, so deeply ingrained. Not only did Never-Despising-Anyone never despise but he actively honored and encouraged.

[10] Dorotheos, *Discourses*, 136.

Dorotheos argues that love does not scrutinize the faults of others but rather covers and screens them, discreetly hiding them from view.[11] Needless to say, we have to be very careful about such language, recognizing all the harmful ways of covering over the faults of others. Often a spirit of collusion, complicit secrecy hides abuses that need to come to light to be rectified. Dorotheos is speaking of the kind of love shown by mature monks, seasoned desert fathers and mothers who suffer with the weak and seek to patiently build them up. Dorotheos likens the sort of pastoral patience he intends to that of a fisherman who knows when to slacken the line and when to reel in the exhausted catch. Importantly, he notes that in extending this patience a monk both protects the erring brother or sister and prevents them from harming anyone else.

To illustrate what he means by hiding the sins of another, he tells the story of Abba Ammonas sitting on the barrel in which he knows the woman is hiding. "By his consideration for his brother he not only protected him after God but corrected him when the right moment came. For when they were alone he laid on him the hand with which he had thrown the others out, and said, 'Have a care for yourself, brother.' Immediately the other's conscience pricked him and he was stricken with remorse, so swiftly did the mercy and sympathy of the old man work upon his soul."[12]

Dorotheos speaks of cultivating "tenderness" toward our neighbor, a word Pope Francis has often invoked. It has a double sense. If I have an injured muscle and the area is "tender," it is sore, sensitive to the touch. If I behave "with tenderness," extend it to another, I show the same care to avoid further injury that I take with my own tender muscle.

[11] Dorotheos, *Discourses*, 136.

[12] Dorotheos, *Discourses*, 137.

Dorotheos invokes the Pauline image of the one body, stressing that we are members of one another. If one of our limbs were injured, or even turned septic, he writes, we would not casually hack it off, but rather tend to it with care and take every possible measure to restore it to health. Stressing that because we are one body, "each one according to his means should take care to be at one with everyone else." He states that "the more one is united to his neighbor the more he is united to God."[13] This is a union at the level of shared life, before and beneath our storylines. Developing a truly contemplative prayer is the surest way to live from this level and gain distance from those stories.

To illustrate his claim that "the more one is united to his neighbor the more he is united to God," Dorotheos concludes his discourse on not judging with the memorable image of a wheel. If the world is a circle and God is the center, with spokes running out to the rim, the nearer we draw to God at the center, the nearer we come to the other spokes of the wheel, where the further from the center we drift, the further we are from one another. Not judging means turning toward and not away from another, suffering with and patiently working to heal them, slackening the line again and again, until the exhausted fish is content to be reeled in. Judging pulls too hard and snaps the line, or even deliberately cuts the line in anger. It turns away from and not toward. The "fisherman" must have the spiritual maturity and liberty of spirit to take on him or herself the burden of the other's affliction and the outcome is by no means guaranteed.

There is a story of a troublesome brother who was about to be expelled from the community. A holy and revered elder begged the brothers to let him stay and to live alongside him in his cell. For weeks he put up with all kinds of

[13] Dorotheos, *Discourses*, 138.

abuse, responding with unfailing calm. But in time it became clear the brother was too troubled and simply had to leave. In real world situations too, there is a need at times for protective force. It's just that these are so much rarer than we imagine. Addicted to violence, we look for the least excuse to pounce on another. Similarly, each day we are tempted in ways great and small to judge others: to run them down, condemn them unjustly, or despise them.

If Dorotheos and the desert tradition are right that nothing so "angers" God or leads to our spiritual ruin so effectively as judging others then the challenge before us is daunting. The habit of judging ourselves and others harshly is so deeply ingrained and is completely integral to the ecosystem of the false self. However ephemeral, we dread the disappearance of this sense of self and desperately reinforce the mirage by judging. We feel real for a moment, more definite, when we put another down and so, implicitly, build ourselves up.

We are so steeped in rivalry at times we barely know it's there. It can be subtle. Considering the contemporary landscape we can be like Anthony who, when he "saw all the snares of the devil spread out everywhere, sighed, and asked God how anyone could ever avoid them. God answered him, 'Humility. It is humility that enables you to escape them all!' And what is more astonishing, he added, 'They cannot even touch you.'"[14] To be humble is to see clearly. We don't judge ourselves but leave judgment to God so hold neither an inflated nor deflated sense of our worth. We see together the goodness and intrinsic dignity of our original nature and the extent of our brokenness, all the ways our conditioned reactivity tries to highjack our highest aspirations. A humble person wades simply into complex situations. Since not only wrath and judging but all the passions

[14] Dorotheos, *Discourses*, 96.

work by dividing us over and against others, the humility that plants us firmly with and for all prevents them from gaining a foothold. There's no longer a "self," in the sense of an entity contrived over against an "other," for the passions to hook onto.

Humility

Dorotheos begins a discourse on humility: "One of the Fathers used to say, 'Before anything else we need humility: a being ready to listen whenever a word is spoken to us, and to say, "I submit," because through humility every device of the enemy, every kind of obstacle is destroyed.' "[15] We need humility "before anything else," otherwise the virtues we develop become a cause for pride. This humility is fundamentally a willingness to listen, an openness to being "struck" by the word. In effect a word is continually being spoken to us, each moment we are given just what we need, so humility means responsiveness. Not managing storylines about how things are, not sifting or photoshopping life to make it better or worse.

Humility moves with confidence on the basis of things as they are, working within the limits of life in a body, life in time, finding guidance and possibility in these very limits. Each moment brings an opening, an offer, and we "submit" to the unvarnished reality of the moment, dark and light, determined to play along because in this way the obstacles that block the free expression of our best self are dissolved. As one of the *Sayings* has it, "Obedience responds to obedience. When someone obeys God, God obeys his request."[16]

[15] Dorotheos, *Discourses*, 94.

[16] *The Sayings of the Desert Fathers: The Alphabetical Collection*, trans. Benedicta Ward, CS 59 (Collegeville, MN: Cistercian Publications, 1984), 150.

Our deepest heart's desire and "the will of God" are one. "I submit" to the whole and renounce the ever-present temptation to spin-doctor the facts. When we're not trying to protect some sacrosanct self-portrait, the Accuser has nowhere to get a foothold.

"Consider well, brothers, how great is the power of humility. Consider how great is the spiritual energy behind saying, 'Pardon me.'"[17] Earlier we touched on the idea of active love in *The Brothers Karamazov*, the willingness to be responsible to all for everything. While of course there are misguided ways of taking the blame or taking responsibility for the feelings or actions of others, the kind of spiritual freedom envisioned by Zosima (and Dorotheos) is that of Jesus graciously "overaccepting" the guilt and scorn of the world.

There's a striking account of a modern Japanese Zen monk who, as part of his training, was sent to beg each day in a nearby village. On his route was a seamstress who for some reason was completely "triggered" by seeing this monk show up at her doorstep, begging. She would curse and yell and throw water at him. The monk skulked off not knowing what to do and eventually asked a more experienced monk to trade routes with him. He watched from hiding as the monk bowed courteously and accepted the insults day after day. Finally, after a particularly abusive attack, the monk looked at the woman and said, "Negative relationships, too, are relationships." The woman broke down in tears and from that day on wove garments for the monks and contributed generously. This is a powerful example of what Gabriel Marcel called "creative fidelity," keeping our door open even when the other person is slamming

[17] Dorotheos, *Discourses*, 95.

theirs in our face over and over. There was nowhere in the older monk for the woman's rage to get a hold.[18]

Dorotheos describes humility as a way to cut short our spiritual journey, to bypass the various obstacles thrown up by the Adversary: "by lowliness, all his attacks and devices are brought to nothing." Far from making us a passive doormat, such an attitude springs from a place of great freedom and creativity, a practice that refreshes and energizes instead of sapping our strength in competing for trifles. Still, texts like the following need to be interpreted: "Humility does not grow angry and does not anger anyone."[19] "Anger" here means essentially wrath and the desire for revenge. In this same passage Dorotheos specifies anger as the sort of thing one feels when someone threatens our food supply or cache of riches. As a passion, anger means something intrinsically askew and selfish.

As we've seen, anger as a healthy impulse has the sense of a "zeal for justice" that motivates us to overcome our fear and correct an injustice. That surge of adrenalin can be discerned and directed, we can ride the wave and use it to bring about good. When anger is allowed to fester, when it is stirred up simply so the momentary burst of empowerment it provides can bolster our fragile ego, it becomes a poison. Even still, the feeling of anger needs to be distinguished from the vengeful intentions and actions it can breed. In no way would Dorotheos suppress or deny the presence of wrath in our hearts. The devil loves to shame us into silence, into not sharing our darkness with a trusted other. Anger as an instinctive feeling needs to be rocked and cradled, cared for with tenderness, precisely so that it won't highjack our lives.

[18] Winifred Bird, "The Counselor," *Tricycle* (Spring 2014).

[19] Dorotheos, *Discourses*, 95.

Dorotheos continues: "If a painful experience comes to a humble man, straightway he goes against himself, straightway he accuses himself as the one worthy of punishment, and he does not set about accusing anyone or putting the blame on anyone else."[20] The humble man "goes against" his tendency to defend and protect his ego and instead of "resisting an evildoer" and reacting to evil with evil, overcomes evil with good by willingly taking the fault on himself. He overaccepts the blame as though it was his, and in this way escapes the deep and subtle tendency to react in kind, to justify and defend himself whether from fear or pride. "For the rest he goes on his way untroubled, undepressed, in complete peace of mind, and so he has no cause to get angry or to anger anyone else."[21] This makes it clear the humble person is not stifling their rage by an act of will. Rather, with long practice, the knot of self has been loosened and perhaps untied altogether. Serene and peaceful, at home in himself, such a one "has no cause" to grow angry.

A wise elderly monk in my community said once, in a discussion about conflict, that if we kept ourselves recollected we would be much less likely to flare up in a dispute. It can almost seem circular. Be at peace and you won't get upset! Not so helpful. But the more we cultivate interior space and care for inflamed passions while they are raw, before they fester, the easier it becomes to respond to life in a fresh and creative way. When we do react we catch it more quickly and find a way to turn things to good. So we must "seek peace, and pursue it" (Ps 34:14). The value of living with balance and equanimity can't be overstated, and it radiates out to others: "Keep your heart at peace and a multitude around you will be saved" (St. Seraphim).

[20] Dorotheos, *Discourses*, 96.
[21] Dorotheos, *Discourses*, 96.

Anger

In a treatise titled "On Rancor and Animosity," Dorotheos goes into some detail distinguishing degrees and kinds of anger, from full-blown rage to subtle, lingering shades of resentment. He underlines the importance of cutting off resentment while it is fresh: "If, from the beginning, you take the blame when you are reproached, without trying to justify yourself or making counter-charges and so repaying evil for evil, you will be delivered from all these ills. This is why I always say to you: when a passion arises, when it is young and feeble, cut it off, lest it stiffen and cause you a great deal of trouble. It is one thing to pluck out a small weed and quite another thing to uproot a great tree."[22] A certain amount of inner quiet is needed to become aware of these first stirrings of the passions, and in this sense "keeping our heart at peace" provides the clarity to fully feel and take note of often subtle feelings so we can take care of them before they grow.

Dorotheos closes his discussion of rancor by stressing the need for continual application to the task of actually working with the passions and not just reading about it. "For what man wishing to learn a trade can master it by verbal instructions alone? No! Always he has to start by doing—and doing it wrong—making and unmaking, until, little by little, working patiently and persevering, he learns the trade while God looks on at his labor and his humility and works with him."[23] In the difficult and delicate craft of working through conflict we can be confident that if we apply ourselves humbly and persistently it will get easier and we will gain real ground. Few things are more satisfying

[22] Dorotheos, *Discourses*, 151.

[23] Dorotheos, *Discourses*, 154.

than after turmoil, much prayer, and many awkward failures to find yourself responding freely and well to a situation where you once would have leapt to judgment.

CHAPTER FIVE

Love

There's a legend about St. Isaac of Syria that he was once made bishop against his wishes. Drawn from desert solitude, on virtually his first day in office he was hearing a case between two disputants, both Christians in the local community:

> One of them was demanding the return of a loan: "If this man refuses to pay back what belongs to me, I will be obliged to take him to court." Isaac said to him: "Since the Holy Gospel teaches us not to take back what has been given away, you should at least grant this man a day to make his repayment." The man answered, "Leave aside for the moment the teachings of the Gospel." Then Isaac said: "If the Gospel is not to be present, what have I come here to do?" And seeing that the office of bishop disturbed his solitary life, "the holy man abdicated from his episcopacy and fled to the holy desert of Skete."[1]

Isaac refuses to judge by any standard other than the gospel and withdraws rather than betray it.

[1] Hilarion Alfeyev, *The Spiritual World of Isaac the Syrian*, CS 175 (Collegeville, MN: Cistercian Publications, 2000), 27.

As in so many other respects Isaac brings the riches of the desert tradition to an especially fruitful development, so too his writings continue the desert emphasis on the way of not judging.

Like Dorotheos, Isaac sees true humility as the key to not judging. "The current of a stream runs swiftly in a narrow place, and likewise the force of anger whenever it finds a place in our mind. The man who has acquired humility in his heart is dead to this world. He who is dead to the world has died to the passions."[2] Judging both arises from and causes further constriction. If the mind is like an artery, blockages occur. Humility is like spiritual nitroglycerin that relaxes and widens the space around the block so blood can circulate. If the arteries grow wider over time most bits of plaque that come along won't be large enough to create a block and will simply flow through. So when we have "died to the passions" they may still break loose but will have nowhere to lodge and become an obstacle.

Although it requires vigilance and patience, if we learn not to react to the passions with passion they eventually dissolve; and almost right away our relation to them changes, and we find ourselves with breathing room. We make way for the passions, feel them to the full, but without reacting. The humble person is unobstructed and able to express him or herself expansively where the passionate are easily blocked: "As the flame of fire cannot be checked from rising upward, so the prayers of the merciful are not hindered from ascending to Heaven." Likewise, God himself cannot be blocked from expressing his mercy in the world: "Just as a strongly flowing spring is not obstructed by a

[2] Isaac of Syria, *The Ascetical Homilies of Saint Isaac the Syrian*, trans. Holy Transfiguration Monastery (Boston: MA, Holy Transfiguration Monastery Publications, 2011), 379–80.

handful of dust, so the mercy of the Creator is not stemmed by the vices of His creatures."[3]

Isaac distinguishes between the humility born of reverence and that born of fervent love. Where a person marked by the first is characterized by modesty and restraint, "the man humbled because of joy is possessed of great exuberance and an open and irrepressible heart." As he writes, "Love knows not shame" and so "does not know to give a form of propriety to her members. Love is naturally unabashed and oblivious of her measure."[4] It's worth recalling that this bolder, more expressive sort of humility is the one the fathers have in view when they imagine the stance of not judging and not the sort of fearful, self-deprecating posture too often associated with "humility." True humility is self-forgetful. "Self-sacrifice," by contrast,very often contains a good deal of "self." That is, one part of the self is reinforced by the restraint of another, and a fundamental selfishness becomes spiritualized and pushed from view.

A Handful of Sand

Earlier, in connection with *The Brothers Karamazov*, we touched on Isaac's powerful image of the sins of the entire world as no more than a handful of sand in comparison with the vast ocean of divine mercy. The original passage reads: "As a grain of sand cannot counterbalance a great quantity of gold, so in comparison God's use of justice cannot counterbalance His mercy. As a handful of sand thrown into the great sea, so are the sins of all flesh in comparison with the mind of God."[5] Christians have tended to imagine

[3] Isaac, *Homilies*, 244.
[4] Isaac, *Homilies*, 245.
[5] Isaac, *Homilies*, 379.

God as torn between his desire to show mercy and a stern demand for justice, even to the point of requiring the torture and death of his Son to somehow balance the books. But it's our desire that is split and we imagine God in our own image. The divine itself is simple beyond anything we can conceive. As Paul writes of Christ, "He was never anything but 'Yes'" (see 2 Cor 1:19). There is no division, no "tension" in God. We experience his presence and action variously in line with our own changeable condition. God cannot help being faithful. He is always himself, unconditioned and unconditional love.

Isaac pictures the "justice" of God as a sand-grain in comparison with the vast treasure hoard of his mercy. Imagine mountains of gold with a tiny speck on a single coin. Although rhetorically set in contrast, in effect, as with the handful of sand and the ocean, Isaac is using a comparison to say there is no comparison; and, I would suggest, no contradiction. Earlier we raised the question of which outcome better satisfied our need for justice: when the murderer who had taken the life of our loved one went to the electric chair unrepentant, or escaped punishment but came to see and feel deeply the irreparable harm they had done and were genuinely repentant. While neither outcome restores the murdered victim, most I think, would prefer that the killer live with the pain and regret of knowing the suffering he'd caused, the goodness of the life he'd destroyed, than simply to suffer violence scoffing. Always courteous and discreet, respecting the freedom of his creatures, God works for this second sort of outcome and uses punishment minimally. In other words, instead of seeing justice and mercy here as opposites, we can understand mercy as a fuller and more satisfying form of justice.

With the image of the ocean and the handful of sand, the challenge is to keep the vast sea of divine goodness as our horizon when we tend so easily to fixate on this or that grain until it fills our vision, a speck in our eye, perhaps, that appears as a wood beam in the eye of another. To say there is no comparison between the sum of human sin and the goodness of God is not meant to diminish sin so much as to remind of how boundless God's mercy is. When in a similar (non-) comparison Paul says, "The sufferings of this present time are not worth comparing with the glory about to be revealed to us" (Rom 8:18), he speaks in the next breath of a terrible cosmic anguish. These however are seen as birth pangs for a new life so exquisite it's of a completely different order to the pain that preceded it.

Similarly, Jesus taught, "When a woman is in labor, she has pain because her hour has come. But when her child is born, she no longer remembers the anguish because of the joy of having brought a human being into the world" (John 16:21). When suffering bears fruit and gives life, its meaning is transformed. In contrast to such fruitfulness: "As a man who sows in the sea and expects to reap a harvest, so is he who remembers wrongs and prays"; and "The prayer of him who remembers wrongs is a seed upon a stone. An unmerciful ascetic is a barren tree."[6]

Simone Weil wrote aptly that "Attention is the rarest and the purest form of generosity."[7] So often our *way* of encountering others communicates more than the "content." "If you give something to one in need, let the cheerfulness of your face precede your gift, and comfort his sorrow with kind words. When you do this, by your gift the gladness of his mind surpasses even the needs of his body."[8] That is, our need to be treated with dignity is in some ways more

[6] Isaac, *Homilies*, 379, 382.

[7] Simone Weil, *A Life, Simone Pétrement*, trans. Raymond Rosenthal (New York: Pantheon, 1976), 462.

[8] Isaac, *Homilies*, 381.

fundamental and urgent than our need for food and water. Directly after this passage Isaac writes: "On the day when you open your mouth and speak ill of someone, even though your thought urged you to say something that seemed correct and for edification, reckon yourself as dead to God and void of all your works. For what need has a man to demolish his own house and set aright that of his companion?"[9] The mentality of judging is set in contrast to that of respectful and attentive presence. However good our intention, we fail to really meet the other as they are. Locked in such a skewed perspective, nothing we do or say can bear fruit. We blind ourselves by judging in order to correct the vision of another. We can't be respectfully, attentively *present* to another when trapped in the mind of judgment. Presence to another as they are constitutes the stance of not judging. This will be seen further in the discussion of the role of contemplative prayer and not judging.

When we suffer on behalf of another, Isaac writes, even suffering the temptation to pass judgment, we become in a sense martyrs and confessors: "On the day when you are pained in some way, either in body or in mind, for the sake of any man, be he good or evil, reckon yourself as a martyr on that day, and as one who suffers for Christ's sake and is deemed worthy of confession."[10] To reframe the voluntary endurance of pain caused by another as a kind of martyrdom means that we take on suffering within the perspective of faith, and unite ourselves with the Christ who underwent such torments in a spirit of free surrender.

Isaac underlines the challenge of suffering not just for the righteous but even and especially on behalf of the unjust: "For remember that Christ died for sinners, not for

[9] Isaac, *Homilies*, 381.

[10] Isaac, *Homilies*, 381.

the just. See how great a thing it is to grieve for wicked men and to benefit sinners even more than the righteous! The Apostle brings this to mind, as something worthy of wonder."[11] We are invited to grieve over those who are "wicked," to grieve for the harm they cause others certainly, and also for the harm they do to themselves.

Psychology has begun to study the "moral injury" we suffer when we harm others, the ways our conscience and inner life become damaged by violating our values. As we've seen, we sin in accord with the ways we have ourselves been harmed and only drive ourselves further into isolation and misery by acting out against others. To grieve and lament the harm done by another means to feel it to the full in a clear-eyed fashion, without reacting in kind. While a vulnerable and apparently weak response it can be the most truly free one and so, very powerful. Christ came to heal the sick not the healthy, and as Isaac's allusion to Romans (5:7-8) reminds, "while we still were sinners." That is, "God proves his love for us in that while we still were sinners Christ died for us," and we are called in turn to extend compassion to those still locked in sin.

"This Is My Body"

Isaac enjoins a gospel approach of non-retaliation in provocative terms: "Be persecuted, but persecute not; be crucified, but crucify not; be wronged, but wrong not; be slandered, but slander not. Have clemency, not zeal, with respect to evil."[12] For the desert fathers, to undergo injury without revenge or complaint is the height of virtue and something completely impossible to us without grace. It is

[11] Isaac, *Homilies*, 381.
[12] Isaac, *Homilies*, 382.

the crown of a life of grace when we can endure accusation and not react in kind, or even, in certain cases, defend ourselves. It is not a matter of thwarting the impulse to revenge by willpower but rather the fruit of a life in deep, prayerful union with the Crucified where there is no longer us and them but one life in and through all, willingly taking to itself all suffering. Imagine for a moment, Christ saying of the body you call your own, the very body you sense in this moment, with all its history of trauma, and illness, with its current tension, fatigue, and hunger: "This is my body." Imagine Christ, the Word, the risen Christ, taking to himself the suffering you hold in your flesh and declaring, "This is my body, I take it to myself and make it my own. This is my body, given for you. I take on your suffering and make it my own so that it may become for you a way to freedom, a way to know a love beyond imagining."

Now imagine this same cosmic Christ saying this from within each body, every person around you, those you love, those you find hard to bear, "This too is my body, given for you." Then the universe is seen as cruciform. All the suffering of each creature acquires a new dimension, a eucharistic meaning in which all participate. There is one life, within and through all, undergoing all. There is one suffering and it is first of all his suffering within and through us. Left to ourselves we cannot bear even the slightest insult or injury while in union with divine love we can "endure all things."

In lines Dostoevsky would adapt in *The Brothers Karamazov*, Isaac describes a merciful heart as follows: "It is the heart's burning for the sake of the entire creation, for men, for birds, for animals, for demons, and for every created thing; and by the recollection and sight of them the eyes of a merciful man pour forth abundant tears."[13] It is a

[13] Isaac, *Homilies*, 491.

universal compassion since all life is interwoven; "every thing that lives is holy."[14] Isaac continues: "From the strong and vehement mercy which grips his heart and from his great compassion, his heart is humbled and he cannot bear to hear or to see any injury or slight sorrow in creation. For this reason he offers up prayers with tears continually even for irrational beasts, for the enemies of the truth, and for those who harm him, that they be protected and receive mercy. And in like manner he even prays for the family of reptiles because of the great compassion that burns without measure in his heart in the likeness of God."[15] Such a person is completely vulnerable and undefended. Through him the tenderness of God finds expression in the world.

The vision of universal mercy pervades *The Brothers Karamazov*: "Until one has indeed become the brother of all, there will be no brotherhood."[16] Recalling how God sees the actions of all clearly and that he is all powerful, Isaac reminds, "You, however, have not been appointed to decree vengeance upon men's deeds and works, but rather to ask for mercy for the world, to keep vigil for the salvation of all, and to partake in every man's suffering, both the just and sinners."[17] The role of the contemplative is to become a conduit of divine mercy. The monk does not abandon the human family but, to paraphrase Evagrius, "goes apart from all for the sake of all." Having received great mercy himself, he plunges into the depths of the human condition, "to partake in every man's suffering" by fully tasting his own.

[14] William Blake, *The Poetry and Prose of William Blake* (Garden City, NY: Doubleday 1965), 50.

[15] Isaac, *Homilies*, 491.

[16] Fyodor Dostoevsky, *The Brothers Karamazov: A Novel in Four Parts with Epilogue*, trans. Richard Pevear and Larissa Volokhonsky (New York: Farrar, Straus and Giroux, 1990), 303.

[17] Isaac, *Homilies*, 457.

Having received abundant mercy, he becomes a wellspring of grace and peace, shining a light in the darkest caverns of the human heart. He keeps "vigil for the salvation of all," even and especially those who are most forsaken.[18]

The reference to the salvation of all is surely not accidental. Bracketing a full discussion of universal salvation, we can note in passing how our present attitude changes the moment we allow that all may ultimately be saved. As long as we're imagining some ultimate separation of Us and Them, our addiction to conflict remains safely grounded. If ultimately ALL will be together, after suitable stints in Purgatory, gazing on the face of God forever, it's harder to lose sight of the redeemable kernel in even our most deplorable adversary. Each person expresses a unique, irreplaceable facet of the divine, however disfigured—and can't be dismissed or reduced to their worst behavior.

Isaac enjoins us to "let a merciful heart preside over your entire discipline" and to prevent evil from coming to another through our agency.[19] We are even to rescue the evil man from evil to the degree that we can. The challenge is fundamentally to "overcome evil with good" (Rom 12:21). He writes: "Conquer evil men by your gentle kindness, and make zealous men wonder at your goodness. Put the lover of justice to shame by your compassion. With the afflicted be afflicted in mind." The "zealous" and "lover of justice" here suggest those bent on heartless punishment and revenge, without empathy for the plight of those they condemn. "Instead of an avenger, be a deliverer. Instead of a faultfinder, be a soother. Instead of a betrayer, be a martyr. Instead of a chider, be a defender."[20]

[18] Isaac, *Homilies*, 457.
[19] Isaac, *Homilies*, 457.
[20] Isaac, *Homilies*, 457.

On the one hand, dramatic acts of gratuitous mercy cannot in any way be forced or prescribed. They arise freely in response to the free gift of grace. In Jesus' parable, the Good Samaritan did not obey a law in ministering to the victim; he was not under obligation to help every person in distress; but he encountered this particular man wounded at the side of the road and he was moved to act. This is part of the sense of Simone Weil's view, mentioned earlier, that we ought to do only those good actions which we cannot not do. We can't compel ourselves to perform works of mercy beyond our measure.

On the other hand, we cannot remain locked in retribution and *realpolitik*, the limits of a "natural" order because grace can't be compelled. Weil observes that as spiritual practice matures the scope of those things we cannot not do expands. It may be something like work as an artist. We could say we ought to make only those poems or paintings we cannot not make, that proceed from an interior ripeness and abundance. Yet we don't sit on our hands waiting for inspiration. There's a certain amount of practice, play, sketching and so on, that disposes us to receive the free gift. We can turn our sails to the wind, steer the boat into the current. So in our life with others, keeping watch over the heart, renouncing judgment in small ways throughout the day, prepares us to freely show mercy in more challenging ways when the occasion arrives. "Whoever is faithful in a very little is faithful also in much" (Luke 16:10).

Isaac underlines that mercy by definition goes beyond conventional human justice. "If the merciful man does not rise above what is just, he is not merciful. That is to say, he is merciful who not only shows mercy to others by giving from his own means, but who also suffers injustice from others with joy, voluntarily; and who not merely keeps and requires justice in his dealings with his fellow men, but also shows them mercy."[21] To give from our abundance to those in need, while typically described as an "act of mercy," is in fact simple justice. The gratuitous "extra" of mercy is shown in suffering injustice, willingly and even with joy. Again, such joyful suffering cannot be compelled or forced, by oneself or another, but arrives as the overflow of mercy received from God and delights in the opportunity to "pay it forward." This runs so counter to our ingrained retaliatory conditioning that only by immersion in the memory of divine goodness and the deliberate intention to watch for and take up the opportunities that arise, however small, to stretch the muscle of not judging, can we hope to grow in this direction. This is what Dorotheos calls the "work of all works" and, as he underlines, it is only by continual application and frequent failure that we progress.

Justice

This last passage from Isaac brings out the broader question of how the order of human justice sits alongside the gratuity of grace, the gift and challenge of the gospel. Isaac says the merciful person "not merely" keeps and requires justice *but also* shows mercy, which suggests mercy as a kind of overflow or superabundance, a "more" that completes and surpasses the order of justice in a higher fulfillment. Not a supersession of justice but a fuller sense to the meaning of justice. In line with the suggestion above that the work of the "active" or moral life is like that of an artist, we can dispose ourselves to receive the gift when it comes, but any effort to force or compel it closes the channel by which we'd receive. Not because God or the Muse is some vengeful tyrant but because the mentality of fear and arrogance that would try to lock in the gift as our own is inimical to the

[21] Isaac, *Homilies*, 142.

free spirit of play in which it could find expression. Manna stored overnight becomes rotten and filled with maggots. The best athletes both put in long hours of practice, train harder than the rest, and dispose themselves to receive the free gift of the "flow state" in which something extra animates their performance. Moralism, perfectionism, and taking oneself too seriously cramp and constrain just as much as laxity drains away our potential.

Isaac goes on to speak of "overcoming" justice by mercy and contrasts the commands and rewards of the Law with those of the gospel. The Law, too, requires us to show care for the poor and forbids injustice, "But the perfection of the Gospel's dispensation commands the following: 'Give to every man that asketh of thee, and of him that taketh away thy goods ask them not again.' "[22] This is another dimension of the saying of St. Seraphim we considered earlier, "Keep your heart at peace and a multitude around you will be saved." If what we most care about is not some private state of inner quiescence we jealously guard against interruption but an actual experience of dynamic harmony with the source of all that is good, we will be free to give to whoever asks, with nothing to hold onto and nothing to protect, since our treasure lies in the heart "where neither rust nor moth destroy" (see Matt 6:20).

Jesus himself frames his teaching in terms of the gratuitous and "extra" vis a vis the old law. "If you love [only] those who love you, what reward do you have?" (Matt 5:46). He enjoins those who give banquets to invite those who can't repay, in order to accrue a kind of "credit" on the other side. That is, he uses the language of indebtedness and reward to invite us into a way of living where love is its own reward. The freedom of spirit implied by the way of life he demonstrates and enjoins simply wants to express itself

[22] Isaac, *Homilies*, 143.

more and more freely. As St. Bernard says, "Love moves us freely and it makes us free."[23] It moves us according to our life as "no longer slaves but sons." The most gratifying "reward" is the very liberty of spirit in which we gladly give all without remainder, without concern for any reward beyond sharing in the Master's spirit, allowing him to live through us to the full.

If "Attention is the rarest and the purest form of generosity,"[24] a wakeful and recollected heart is inseparable from true compassion. Both, if they are two, involve being at home with our weakness. It requires a wakeful, unjudging heart to see clearly and get close to our weakness, and awareness of our weakness in turn spurs us to watchfulness: "Blessed is the man who knows his own weakness, because this knowledge becomes to him the foundation, the root, and the beginning of all goodness. For whenever a man learns and truly perceives his own weakness, at that moment he contracts his soul on every side from the laxity that dims knowledge, and he treasures up watchfulness in himself."[25]

An intimate awareness of the ways we've been wounded and shaped by those wounds, the knowledge that we have blind spots, that we're fallible, limited, and weak, at any moment one breath, one heartbeat away from death; all of this forms the solid bedrock, "the beginning of all goodness." Truly to get close to our weakness demands not judging. When the spirit of accusation and self-hatred prevails, we can't bear to let the full truth of our misery arise as we know it will provoke within us only wrath and derision.

[23] Paraphrased from Bernard of Clairvaux, *On Loving God*, trans. Robert Walton, CF 13B (Collegeville, MN: Cistercian Publications, 1973), p. 20.

[24] Weil, *A Life, Simone Pétrement*, 462.

[25] Isaac, *Homilies*, 185.

Truly to know, to own and accept the full truth of our poverty with compassion and understanding, is the basis for any goodness we might show to others. If we perform "works of mercy" they are not done from a sense of obligation or in a spirit of condescension, however subtle, but with a felt sense for the dignity of the one we serve. There is essentially one misery, one guilt, and one indomitable Life within us that takes upon itself this suffering. Isaac underlines that knowing just how easily we fool ourselves and fall away, how subtly temptation can skew our thoughts, we are on guard and keep watch with diligence, treasuring up watchfulness. The awareness of how the passions are active within us at any given moment, the pressure they exert to distort our interpretation of events, is what the desert tradition understands by "spiritual discernment," the positive counterpart to "judging," a topic we'll explore further in the next chapter.

For the moment, we can note the connection Isaac makes between humility, recollection, and the merciful heart: " 'A heart that is broken and humbled, God will not despise.' Therefore, as long as the heart is not humbled, it cannot cease from wandering, for humility collects the heart." For Isaac there is both a positive and a negative sense to both contraction and expansion. While the heart moved by love expands boldly, that controlled by slavish fear contracts, stiff and rigid. Yet the slack heart expands in aimless wandering and dispersion where the vigilant are taut, on guard and watchful.

He continues, "But when a man becomes humble, at once mercy encircles him, and then he is aware of Divine help, because it finds a certain power and assurance moving in itself."[26] Not judging, not putting ourselves in the place

[26] Isaac, *Homilies*, 185–86.

of God but humbly accepting our weakness, unsurprised, and unscandalized by it, we find we are "encircled" by mercy. We open the pores, long clogged, that can at last absorb the mercy that surrounded us all along. When we are humble we feel "a certain power and assurance" moving within us; we are confident because we are grounded firmly in things as they are and not in a storyline. Humility is like a magnet that keeps us anchored to the earth while, based in fantasy, pride makes us rootless and easily blown away.

In newly discovered writings by Isaac recently translated into English, there are several powerful passages on not judging. Isaac counsels us to keep watch over our thoughts, to guard against judging, as the same person who appears so reprehensible to us now may soon appear in a different light. We mustn't follow thoughts, then, that "show us whatever they like." A loving heart will discreetly cover rather than expose the faults of others. Those who claim to love God while sitting in judgment of their neighbor are fooling themselves. Isaac underscores both their hypocrisy and ignorance. Echoing Dorotheos he states that nothing "angers" God more than monks, supposedly living a penitential life, who judge the sins of others: "There is nothing at which God is so angered, or which is so vexatious in his presence as the person who sits in his cell thinking about his companion, having made his cell the court room where he is the judge who judges the deficiencies of others. And yet he considers himself a penitent and says in prayer 'As I have forgiven, forgive me!' "[27]

[27] Isaac of Nineveh, *Headings on Spiritual Knowledge: The Second Part, Chapters 1–3*, trans. Sebastian Brock (Yonkers, NY: St. Vladimir's Seminary Press, 2022), 53.

Isaac's language here brings out the element of revenge fantasy that so often accompanies the mind of judgment. We are on the bench with the gavel and the one we admonish a groveling defendant. Isaac goes on to ask, if we are judged for judging those who actually harm us, how much more when we judge affairs that take place "at a distance?" He asks, "If you cannot bear to see the deficiencies and weaknesses of others and cannot endure it in your mind, then go off somewhere else." That is, remove yourself instead of casting out others, if you find their faults so hard to bear. "Otherwise, how do you think it is possible for us to see everyone as good when we do not possess stillness?"[28]

At home in ourselves and at rest in God, we see the goodness in each person we encounter. Seeing with the eyes of faith, we are more taken with the unique manifestation of the divine in a human life than we are dismayed by what seems to us to be that image's disfiguration. When our own true self is activated, we more easily intuit and connect with the true self in those around us. Again, we see the close link between stillness and not judging. Indeed, in the prayer of stillness we develop the habit of not judging as we allow thought after thought to arise and dissolve without reaction, opening the book of our hearts before God.

As we've seen, keeping the heart at peace does not mean jealously guarding some private comfort zone over and against encroaching threats but involves precisely the cultivation of a peace in the midst of conflict. If we are at peace we will see things rightly. "Be peaceable and humble, *so that* you may find compassion for everyone." Not judging reinforces and secures peace where judging destroys it. Isaac goes on to note that "circumstances appear in various lights, corresponding to the activity of the heart," to what the heart

[28] Isaac, *Headings*, 53.

is directed toward, whether the good or temptation. "Do not be a reprover or corrector of anyone, and do not be zealous and agitated in your soul."[29] For Isaac, obsessively fixated on the correction of others we close ourselves to deep insight into the kindness of God. This "zealous" state of mind results from and furthers wandering. Far from a permissiveness that simply wants to avoid conflict, the inner clarity of not judging unmasks the distortions of the Accuser. These include a lack of trust in God's power to judge to which we are called to continually defer. The deepest concern for justice holds in view the inherent human goodness of the oppressor and our own fallibility, alongside a confidence in God's way of bringing the unjust to account.

Isaac finds "righteous zeal" to derive either "from pride or stupidity." One possessed of it is either convinced of his own sinlessness and his power to save others (pride) or "imagines he is being a friend of God when he hates sinners." Isaac blasts this last view in the strongest terms: "This is a mentality of utter stupidity, and one that is totally alien to all knowledge of God: such a person does not realize that the saints accepted all kinds of death on behalf of wicked men and murderers in order to bring them to the way of God by means of love." The way of the gospel, the way Jesus himself demonstrated, is to lay down one's life even and especially for those who are undeserving, who have no way to repay the gift. Underlining the christological basis for this provocative view, Isaac writes: "Those who are aware of God's purpose, and have been held worthy to know fully his will, will die for the sake of sinners in the likeness of the Son of God."[30]

[29] Isaac, *Headings*, 54.
[30] Isaac, *Headings*, 54.

Sin as Suffering

God, as Bernard wrote, is "neither offended by our sins nor placated by our penance."[31] God sees our sin not as a blemish or stain he must erase, or an offense he must avenge to restore his honor, but as suffering. He sees the twofold suffering of the one who commits evil: the suffering that gives rise to evil conduct and the suffering that such conduct further entrenches. He sees the suffering we cause ourselves by sinning, the alienation, isolation, and bitterness, despite whatever perceived short-term reward.

Part of not judging is the refusal of the terms set by our assailant. Where overt or indirect retribution involves acting essentially within the frame and according to the terms created by an evildoer, not judging imagines a wider set of possibilities. When we judge, we tend to reduce the other to their action, and reduce their action to sheer wickedness, without context. To see sin as suffering in the deep sense involves more (but not less) than acknowledging that our sin grows from the ways we've been sinned against.

A mystic closer to us in time who holds a view remarkably like that of Isaac is Julian of Norwich. For both, the cross is not God somehow exacting payment or punishing himself for our sins but the revelation of his steadfast unconditioned love, a revelation designed to convince us precisely of the unconditional nature of his love for us and awaken a gratuitous response. In several inspired pages Matthew Potts unpacks Julian's writings. "God, Julian says, 'regards sin as sorrow and suffering for those who love him, to whom he attributes no blame, out of love.' Thus we will be rewarded and comforted for our sinful suffering in God's

[31] Bernard of Clairvaux, *Sentences* 124.3, in *The Parables and The Sentences*, trans. Michael Casey and Francis R. Swietek, CF 55 (Collegeville, MN: Cistercian Publications, 1991), 436.

heavenly company rather than eternally punished for it. Sin does not incur an obligation to suffer; for Julian the sin *is* the suffering. 'Christ has compassion on us because of sin.'"[32]

As sinners who know firsthand the estrangement and self-hatred of having committed sin, we ought all the more to feel for those who cut themselves off from life and goodness by their harmful actions. "Sin is its own worst punishment" (Augustine), a harsher and more destructive one than true justice (which is mercy) demands. In Julian's view, as relayed by Potts, "God has never been angry toward us and never could be . . . Our soul is united to God in God's 'unchangeable goodness'; therefore, 'between God and our soul is neither anger nor forgiveness.' For Julian, a deep love binds us to God, and the notion that that love might somehow be sullied by wrath, let alone need repair through pardon, simply misunderstands the nature of that love."[33] In the parable, the father does not forgive the prodigal because of his stammered prefabricated lines about his unworthiness. He simply loves, and "love covers a multitude of sins" (1 Pet 4:8).

God is not merciful one minute and then wrathful the next like some capricious and tyrannical parent. When his love comes up against sin, it assumes the aspect of forgiveness and compassion. Subjectively, however, the person locked in sin may experience that love as oppressive and imagine a God full of wrath and fury.[34] When exposed to the cold a long time, our extremities grow numb and become frostbitten. If we realize how cold we are and come inside, the warmth that wakens our blood flow into circula-

[32] Matthew Ichihashi Potts, *Forgiveness: An Alternative Account* (New Haven, CT: Yale University Press, 2022), 166.

[33] Potts, *Forgiveness*, 163.

[34] Potts, *Forgiveness*, 164.

tion feels excruciatingly painful. But it's the only way to melt and thaw. We may fear that suffering and prefer to stay numb and freeze. The pain of remorse, of seeing clearly the nature and extent of our sin, how petty and selfish we've been, how we've hurt those we most love, can be excruciating. Only the exquisite warmth after so much cold, the cessation of the frigid wind, the awareness of being loved as we are, allows us to bear it. As we saw earlier, with genuine compunction the two always arise together: knowledge of our misery, awareness of unconditional love for us just as we are in our sin.

Potts underlines the unchanging quality of divine mercy and writes that for Julian,

> forgiveness transforms the sinner rather than God. God has not changed; Christ and the sinner have never been estranged from one another. What has changed is the sinner's vision of God, her understanding of the persistence and intimacy of God's love. Divine forgiveness, on these terms, is not the reacquisition of God's favor but the recognition that God was never angry nor distant in the first place. Forgiveness for Julian does not signify God's change of heart; rather, it signifies the unchanging willingness of God to love God's enemies . . . God is always present in and as love to the sinner; it is the sinner who comes to realize this love in time as forgiveness.[35]

What if we too were to see sin as suffering—not just the result of suffering but an expression of it? If we were to see sin as God sees it . . . This is the perspective to which Isaac invites us with the challenge to "die for the sake of sinners in the likeness of the Son of God." Most often this will be a very little "death" to the ego, a setting aside of our cherished

[35] Potts, *Forgiveness*, 164.

viewpoint, or sitting lightly toward our preference. But as noted above, "Whoever is faithful in a very little is faithful also in much" (Luke 16:10). Attunement to the opportunities that arise each day to practice not judging in small ways lays the groundwork to support more generous responses when, from time to time, the occasion arises.

Looking ahead to the discussion of discernment, I'd like to touch on a few last texts by Isaac. In the first, he writes that one who is without recollection of God in his heart will carry instead suspicion of his neighbor. By contrast, one who honors others out of a spirit of recollection, a contemplative sense of divine presence, will find himself supported on all sides by others "by God's secret command," recalling our discussion of the gospel principle that the one who shows mercy receives it, as though mercy were a sort of two-way door or a channel widened by use. One who shows mercy is alert to and grateful for the ways others help and support him.

Further, where the one who helps and advocates for others finds God himself as his advocate, "He who accuses his brother on account of his evil deeds has God for his own Accuser."[36] It is not that God changes but as we touched on above, our perception of him shifts with our inner state. The scriptures speak of the Spirit as Advocate and Satan as Accuser, and God unfailingly works for the salvation of all, yet "as you judge, so will you be judged" (see Matt 7:2), and a heart given over to suspicion and accusation will find its wrath reflected back to it in the image of an angry God, another dimension of sin being its own worst punishment. To the degree that we judge others harshly we are haunted by the specter of our own judgment, and the face of the merciful one is obscured and distorted.

[36] Isaac, *Homilies*, 363.

Isaac goes on to stress discretion as a mark of loving correction where public accusation is often a mark of envy. He finds retribution totally alien to the nature of a God who is so tenderhearted and compassionate, that if it wouldn't risk compromising our freedom, he might not reprove us at all:

> The man who administers chastisement with a view to healing, chastises with love; but he who seeks vengeance is devoid of love. God chastises with love, not for the sake of revenge—far be it!—but seeking to make whole His image . . . But the man who chooses to consider God an avenger, presuming that in this manner he bears witness to His justice, the same accuses Him of being devoid of goodness. Far be it, that vengeance could ever be found in that Fountain of love and Ocean brimming with goodness! The purpose of His mind is the correction of men; and if it were not that we should be stripped of our free will, perhaps he would not even heal us by reproof.[37]

God seeks to warm and thaw our frostbitten limbs and if that warmth causes pain as the blood starts to circulate, he is not inflicting that pain to punish but rather because it's integral to our healing. Isaac writes that "the pains of love" are the most bitter of all: "I also maintain that those who are punished in Gehenna are scourged by the scourge of love. For what is so bitter and vehement as the punishment of love? I mean that those who have become conscious that they have sinned against love suffer greater torment from this than from any fear of punishment. For the sorrow caused in the heart by sin against love is sharper than any torment that can be." He goes on to describe how love torments sinners as when one feels bitter remorse for having

[37] Isaac, *Homilies*, 364.

injured a friend, but gives joy to those who have been faithful.[38]

Discernment means keeping in view, under the pressure of temptation to judge, that we are all on the same side against both the passions and our common Accuser, who works by dividing us against ourselves. It means giving way to the One who suffers all in and through us, who is "guilty to all for everything," and who sees in sin not an "offense" to be avenged, as though God were some touchy aristocrat demanding a duel, but as "sorrow and suffering."

> Do not hate the sinner. We are, indeed, all laden with guilt. If for the sake of God you are moved to oppose him, weep over him. Why do you hate him? Hate his sins and pray for him, that you may imitate Christ Who was not wroth with sinners, but interceded for them. Do you not see how He wept over Jerusalem? We are mocked by the devil in many instances, so why should we hate the man who is mocked by him who mocks us also? Why, O man, do you hate the sinner? Could it be because he is not so righteous as you? But where is your righteousness when you have no love? Why do you not shed tears over him? But you persecute him. In ignorance some, who are considered to be discerning men, are moved to anger against the deeds of sinners.[39]

Spiritual discernment then can be seen as the true form of which "judgment" is the caricature.

[38] Isaac, *Homilies*, 266.
[39] Isaac, *Homilies*, 387.

CHAPTER SIX

Discernment

The story of King Solomon and the two mothers is a justly famous illustration of discernment (1 Kgs 3:16-28). Both mothers have recently borne children. One claims the other smothered her child in sleep and then replaced her own newborn with the dead child. The other claims the live child is hers. The king calls for a sword and orders the child to be cut in two with half going to each mother. When the one protests, and begs that the child not be killed but given to the other, Solomon recognizes her as the mother and gives her the child.

The decision (a bluff) to cut the child in two and give equal halves to each claimant is a caricature of justice. The good (in this case a child) would be simply an object to be portioned out with no sense of its own life and integrity. The woman who stole the child reveals her envy in her willingness to see the child die, since envy can be described not as wanting what the other has so much as hatred of the other's having it. The actual mother shows the child belongs to her by her willingness to renounce it. She cares more for the life of the child itself than her own claim. Although the prospect of losing the child, especially to such a cruel rival, would have been terrible, she is able to relinquish her part in the rivalry for the sake of the child.

The focus in the story is on the wise discernment of Solomon, whose feint weeds out the impostor. But the mother also makes a discernment, namely that it is better for her child to live without her, even for it to belong to her enemy, than not to live at all. If the initial judgment was carried out and the child cut in two, it is the baby who would be punished. So in retributive schemes generally it is the good at stake that is sacrificed. If we take the bait and fall into the trance of revenge, we fail to be mothers of the good. If we place the good ahead of our own claim to it, if we refuse to insist on our view for the sake of a still broader truth we trust will come to light, we make way for that truth and even show ourselves its mothers.

Although Israel perceives "the wisdom of God" in Solomon's tactic, one could argue, I suppose, that it merely amounts to a clever ploy. The spiritual discernment the desert tradition demonstrates, the discernment that is the true form of which "judging" is a counterfeit, involves the psychological dimension of our life, the thoughts and feelings with which we usually identify, becoming transparent to the spirit. Christian tradition speaks at times not just of body and soul but of body, soul, and spirit. Just as we can gain some sense of the soul (or "psyche") of another only through what they express in their bodies so we can know the spirit only through the psyche. Just as a psychologist could not ignore a patient's body and expect to know anything of her mind, so the spiritual life demands intimate familiarity with the psychological, the full realm of our thoughts and feelings. This perspective avoids both the sort of fundamentalism that would dismiss psychology altogether and the reduction of the spiritual to psychology alone. This last is akin to the stance of the behaviorist who claims everything is physical and the interior an illusion.

In his study of the desert father tradition, the Greek philosopher Stelios Ramfos writes, "[T]he supremely discerning person is one who is transparent rather than critical. Transparency precedes judgment. Where it exists, I am in the presence of God Himself, that is to say, I encounter Him before I come to an awareness of moral obligations."[1] The experience of the spirit is the experience of the psychological realm becoming transparent. The field of thoughts and feelings, and the ever-shifting sense of self they generate are seen suddenly at a distance and as altogether relative. The true self, the whole person I am before thought, before identification, is experienced as a no-self, as a gap or absence, when the sense of self I've lived with as far back as I can remember, is suddenly seen through. The "self" that includes everything is expressed as not judging, not making self by putting one thing against another, by claiming to be this and not that, or judging that another person is one thing and not another.

Direct encounter with the presence of God, the experience of the gratuity of grace, comes before and radically reframes the field of moral obligation. Instead of reacting guiltily to a henpecking superego and forcing ourselves to act in a way that lines up with human convention, the gratuity of grace sparks gratitude and response in kind. "When the eye is sound, the body will be filled with light";[2] and when the spirit is sound, the field of thoughts and feelings grows clear. It's the difference between looking at stained glass windows from outside at night and seeing them sunlit and from within the church.

[1] Stelios Ramfos, *Like a Pelican in the Wilderness: Reflections on the Sayings of the Desert Fathers*, trans. Norman Russell (Brookline, MA: Holy Cross Orthodox Press, 2000), 227.

[2] Thomas Merton, *The Wisdom of the Desert: Sayings from the Desert Fathers of the Fourth Century* (New York: New Directions, 1970), 45.

It's important to reiterate that not judging is not the absence of angry or judgmental thoughts—these can come and go with great frequency. In one desert father saying a young monk complains of distractions, and his abba invites him to open his robe to swallow up the wind—to exhaust distraction being just as impossible. So it is with the distraction of judgmental thoughts. And as we learned in a key saying mentioned earlier, "It's not for sinful thoughts that we're condemned but only for making use of them."[3]

Not judging is not a condition we impose by effort but our natural state before thinking. We need the space of acceptance to fully see and experience the mind of judging. Otherwise, the judge will fear judgment and hide in the shadows. Just as accurate awareness of sin occurs only in the presence of unconditional love, so harmful thoughts are seen clearly in the space of acceptance, the self that "includes everything." Even though the spirit is clear by nature, because it's been overgrown by habit and prejudice we often need another person to provide the open space in which we can hear and come to accept ourselves. Hence the importance the desert tradition places on the role of the elder and the sharing of thoughts. At the outset especially (but further along as well) we need others to model for us the balance and perspective we find hard to bring to our own inner condition. One of Ignatius of Loyola's key tools for discernment was to imagine what we might say to a friend who found themselves in our position. Often we find our counsel would be far kinder than what we offer ourselves.

Acting on and identifying with judgmental thoughts, then, is where the trouble lies. Before exploring further the desert tradition on discernment as the true form of which "judgment" is a corruption, I'd like to touch on a passage

[3] Merton, *Wisdom of the Desert*, 45.

by a kind of early modern desert father, Francois Fenelon (1651–1715), who enjoins a posture of not judging such that we "allow all appearances and all reasons for believing to pass before our eye." He recommends, even with indifferent, everyday matters, judging only when necessary and sitting lightly to our own views. He writes: "In all things judge as little as you possibly can. It is a very simple matter to hold back all decisions that are not necessary for us. This is not lack of resolution. It is a simple distrust of ourselves and a very practical detachment from our own ideas. And this distrust and detachment extend to everything, even to the commonest things."[4]

If we form the habit of responsiveness and not imposing our way in minor matters, it will be easier in weightier ones. Far from paralysis or timidity such an approach makes way for life. We hold a realistic and balanced, not exaggerated, sense of our own fallibility and blind spots and so sit lightly toward views of which we're inclined to feel certain, aware that new angles and elements will come to light. Fenelon continues:

> When we are truly detached, we believe what we ought to believe and we act when necessary with a simple determination and without thinking about ourselves or trusting in ourselves. When there is no necessity, we do not judge, and we allow all appearances and all reasons for believing to pass before our eye. Instead we are so empty of self and of our own opinions that we are always ready to receive light from others. We are willing to believe that we are mistaken, and ready to retrace our steps like a little child whom its mother leads back by the hand.[5]

[4] Francois Fenelon, *The Complete Fenelon*, trans. Robert J. Edmonson and Hal M. Helms (Brewster, MA: Paraclete Press, 2008), 114.

[5] Fenelon, *Complete Fenelon*, 114.

In this way we are self-forgetful instead of self-conscious. We are slow to impose "judgments" that so often are merely a matter of preference and bias. Instead of imposing our view, we step back and allow a fuller spectrum of possibilities to appear. "Empty of self," we are receptive to life and the guidance it brings each moment. Because we are not identified stiffly with a course of action there is no need to double down and insist defensively on steps taken. Instead we have a sense of possibility, of pliability that allows us to revise and reimagine continually in tune with unfolding events. Where judgment brings acrimony and discord, the pliable way brings peace: "This emptiness of spirit, this childlike readiness and willingness to be taught, will bring peace to your heart—peace with yourself and with your neighbor."[6]

Discernment proceeds from and moves toward love. As Ramfos writes, "The aim of discernment is to make sure one's own good does not exist at the expense of someone else's. It is one thing to avoid what harms me personally, and another to distinguish my own good, as a common good, from what is good for me regardless of the consequences to other people." My own good is not just or even primarily mine. "My" life is something I received, not something I chose or created; it's come to me through the care

[6] Fenelon, *Complete Fenelon*, 114. Fenelon's view aligns with our description of the true self as the father between the elder and younger sons in the parable. As his biographer describes, Fenelon believed: "we are to let everything about ourselves, good and bad, 'fall away,' so that it is not 'ours' any longer and is inconsequential (the French is *qu'importe*—what does it matter?). We avoid the religious hypocrisy of self-righteousness on the one hand, when we are good, or, on the other, the despair of self-condemnation (anxious scruples) when we are bad—both of which are forms of self-love"; Peter Gorday, *Francois Fenelon: The Apostle of Pure Love; A Biography* (Brewster, MA: Paraclete Press, 2012), 116.

and dedication of many, inextricably interwoven with the life of all.

A truly spiritual practice will be life-giving for others, self-forgetful not self-absorbed: "*Askesis* is self-defeating the moment it brings grief to others. It becomes an end in itself and instead of opening a person up puts a protective screen around him. The egocentric closing in of asceticism is dispelled by discernment, which seeks to transform it into the grace and joy of giving."[7] To fast in such a way that we become unbearable for others to be around, or neglect our responsibilities in order to tread out our preferred rut of personal devotions, is to reduce spiritual practice and asceticism to an expression of the self-will it's meant to free us from. As though an athlete were to train not to run the best race but from a mechanical attachment to his preferred training regime. Then asceticism becomes a prophylactic that buffers the intensity of life and protects the self from the risks of what lies beyond its control.

The task of discernment is to open this self-protective shell into "the grace and joy of giving" like a wise coach who helps a runner connect with his original passion for the sport. He puts the focus less on adherence to this or that point of instruction and more on the runner learning to find their way into a "flow state" where he spontaneously arrives at peak performance without strain or even perceived effort.

We noted earlier that the "word" supplied in the *Sayings* is a particular counsel offered to a particular person in his or her unique situation, not (usually) a general law or principle. This is brought out in a story where two monks approach their abba with the same issue and receive different advice. One is told to suppress the thought that troubles

[7] Ramfos, *Like a Pelican*, 220.

him, the other to let it come to light. Knowing the character of each, the abba intuits that where the one would likely be overcome by temptation and discouragement the other can grow by allowing his thoughts into the open.

Like Wells's improvisation, obedience demands continual attunement and responsiveness to unique developments as opposed to the rote memorization and performance of lines. Ramfos writes:

> The imposition of moral obligations does not save. What saves is the discerning combination of insistence on the will of God with the capability of each one of us. What is important is the psychological opening of a person, not a particular conformity to the rules. The word "ought" is superfluous to the person who knows the good and lives it. Of course, conformity to rules has its importance and its significance. But the richer we become in our inward lives, the more progress we make and our relationship to the group becomes more free the more the rule with its demands comes to take second place. What has priority is our own truth.[8]

Like Augustine's "Love God and do what you will," a passage like this can sound like or seem to support a certain permissive self-delusion in which we let ourselves off the hook as too mature for adherence to the rules "those others" who are less advanced still require; and of course our capacity for delusion is bottomless, so care is required. Full weight needs to be given to the will of the living God made known to our conscience in unfolding life as opposed to the perceived security of pre-set norms. Also, while we might see the danger in such a view allowing us to do "less," it may be better read in terms of discerning what "more" we undertake.

[8] Ramfos, *Like a Pelican*, 222.

Consider this account of two modern "desert mothers." Catherine Doherty recounts visiting Dorothy Day for the first time in New York where she was running a homeless shelter. The two were going to share the one remaining bed when just before they closed the doors for the night a woman came in, without a nose, and clearly syphilitic. Day told Doherty she could go sleep in the tub, she was going to share the bed with this woman and tend to her. Doherty, who (like Day) was a nurse, pulled her aside and told her the woman was surely syphilitic and could be contagious. Day said firmly, "You need to have faith" and proceeded to sleep beside the woman, comforting her through the night. Christ was present in this woman and Christ would take care of her.[9]

We have a "moral obligation" to care for our health and not subject it to needless risk—and Day would not have thrown caution aside in every case—but in this moment she was moved to go the extra mile. In Weil's terms she "could not not" help without ignoring her heart. Day, or the Good Samaritan, are "struck" as one is struck with wonder or compunction. A monk has been characterized as one who is "willing to be struck." The monastic vocation is a kind of susceptibility to having one's heart broken over and over. This is "the psychological opening of a person" to which Ramfos refers. The heart softens and we grow transparent. There's more and more we cannot not give. When he speaks of the priority of "one's own truth," he means not the label we attach to ourselves in some kind of identitarian sense but that vulnerable affective core that is inexplicably moved, "struck," touched by the gratuity of grace and impelled to respond in kind.

[9] Catherine Doherty, *Fragments of My Life* (Notre Dame, IN: Ave Maria Press, 1979), 108.

Ramfos describes discernment as a spiritual charism distinct from judgment. Where judgment relies on external criteria and operates within the sphere of human thought and feeling, a sphere compromised and confused by "the passions," discernment is born of grace and enjoys some distance from them:

> The criterion of good and evil becomes one of whether the intended action is illicit, which destroys truth and our spiritual realization. Discernment, however, in the way the ascetics view it, has spiritual realization as its aim, and in this sense coincides with a dynamic of existence in which our true self finds its fulfillment. If discernment is a virtue, it is one by which the human person finds the means to go beyond good and evil and in this way, in a manner which transcends reason, to discredit evil.[10]

Imagine Dorothy Day ignoring her gut response and trying to calculate whether to care for the sick woman was "licit"—she would miss the call to go the extra mile. That call is not a matter of obligation, something that can be prescribed but openings arise for gratuitous response and we're moved to act.

Strangely enough, our most free (because gratuitous) actions then are those we "cannot not do." For Day, as for Jesus, to empty herself out coincided with the realization of her heart's desire and her fulfilment as a person—a fulfilment through emptying. Attunement to those moments in which we are called to a more profound kenosis and the willingness to be "poured out as a libation," shattered like the jar of precious nard, allows the move beyond the conventional "good" that is no more than the opposite of evil

[10] Ramfos, *Like a Pelican*, 224.

(even, Simone Weil will say, little better than another form of it!). To "overcome evil with good" demands not responding in kind, reactively, but from a space of interior freedom grounded in the unique experience of the grace we've received, our unique experience of conversion.

Rather than an autonomous subject weighing options, selecting among various paths according to a process of rational calculation, a fuller version of the "truth" is allowed to arise and our own complex motives and biases are brought to light. In a sense, just as the "viewer" of an icon encounters a presence such that they are seen more than they see, so we are discerned more than we actively discern. Ramfos continues: "[T]he discerning person does not locate the good in making choices according to moral rules but conceives of it as the separation of truth from untruth, of darkness from light. He refuses to judge because he understands that all sins are the products of one supreme sin: we love what is false too much to look God in the eyes. Sin is not that we do what is forbidden. It is that we do not live in the light of truth."[11]

What the desert tradition refers to as our "passions," damaged, largely unconscious drives and biases, generate storylines, narratives of how things are, to which we become fiercely attached, with which we become identified. The primal fear of disappearance can be triggered by something that calls into question the "story" (ideology, account, self-image) in which we've become so invested. Often, as we'll see in the chapter to come, we are at least as attached to negative self-images as grandiose ones. We carry a "bright" shadow of unrealized possibility imprisoned within the stiff prefabricated images we hold of who we are and what we can be. We forget that "his power, now at work

[11] Ramfos, *Like a Pelican*, 226–27.

in us, can do immeasurably more than we ask or imagine" (see Eph 3:20-21). Discernment involves an effective faith awareness of our being made "in the image of God" and our status as "no longer slaves but sons," no longer servants but friends. The field of our conditioned thoughts and feelings has to some degree grown transparent and we grow sensitive to how easily and subtly our view can be distorted.

Wakefulness

"Abba Agathon was asked, 'Which is greater: physical labor or interior vigilance?' and he answered, 'A person is like a tree; physical labor is the leaves, interior vigilance the fruit. Given that which is written, "every tree not bearing good fruit will be cut down and cast into the fire" [Matt 7:19], it is clear that our entire concern is with the fruits, meaning the vigilance of the mind; but there is also need of the protection and ornamentation the leaves provide: these are physical labor.' "[12] The image of the tree reinforces the prominent theme in the desert fathers that external practice is only a means to an end, to secure inner watchfulness and purity of heart. The leaves too are an expression of the tree and serve to enhance and protect its beauty as the practices of monastic life (fasting, vigils, psalmody and so on) express and preserve its inner spirit. If we can sense all the elements of a situation and all the ways the different sides of ourselves are responding, the right thing to do (and, by grace, the motivation to do it), very often will emerge like a ripe fruit, an obvious next step. This requires waiting,

[12] *The Book of the Elders: Sayings of the Desert Fathers; The Systematic Collection*, trans. John Wortley, CS 240 (Collegeville, MN: Cistercian Publications, 2012), 145–46.

listening, attentiveness to life, and keeping watch over the heart. But it's both more natural and effective than self-consciously fretting over which path to choose, the illusion of the autonomous ego buttressing itself by forcing a way.

As we've seen, on the cross God takes the risk of loving unconditionally, gratuitously, hoping to awaken a similarly free and gratuitous response. It may or may not succeed. For the desert fathers too there is no guarantee that the way of not judging will inspire change. Along with the many stories where dramatic acts of non-judging provoke a change of heart in a monk who's off-track, there is this account:

> Abba Daniel also told how when Abba Arsenius was at Scete, there was a monk there who was stealing the elders' goods. Abba Arsenius took him into his cell, wishing to win him over and to give the elders some respite. He said to him, "I will provide you with whatever you desire, only just do not steal." He gave him gold, coins, clothes, and everything he needed, but he went off and stole again. So the elders expelled him when they realized that he had not stopped, saying, "If a brother is found at fault through some weakness, he should be tolerated; but if he steals and does not stop when he is warned, expel him, for he is both damaging his soul and disturbing everybody in the place."[13]

The story can also be considered in a certain tension with those in which monks help robbers to plunder their goods; here it is a fellow monk who is addicted to stealing. There is an interesting distinction between "weakness," which should be tolerated, and a stubborn persistence in wrong-doing where the monk is so in the grip of a passion that he apparently cannot be helped . . . or at least not right away

[13] *The Book of the Elders*, 148.

or in the monastic setting. Sometimes it can be counter-productive for a person to remain in their community. We're not told how Abba Arsenius responds; does he agree to the decision of the elders? The point of the episode seems to be both to show Arsenius going the extra mile and to say that sometimes even that is not enough. At least not right away. Sometimes such acts of kindness have a "sleeper effect" and it's only years later that their full meaning and impact becomes clear.

Just as for Isaac of Syria, if we can't prevent ourselves from judging others harshly then we ought to remove ourselves from the scene, so here if a person's actions are poisoning the communal ecosystem beyond what it can absorb, and they persist in causing harm despite the kind of generosity Arsenius extends, then a separation may be called for. The urge to punish and exclude is so deeply ingrained and at times so subtle that great care must be taken in discerning the best course. The discriminating person will be alert to the desire for retribution.

Spiritual discernment operates from faith in the God "who loved me and gave himself for me" (Gal 2:20). We are convinced of the reality of divine, unconditional love, hear the competing voices of fear, self-interest, and the storylines they generate, and can steer accordingly. We renounce our own judgment and defer to that of a God to whom "everything is naked and exposed" (see Heb 4:13). We are discerned more than we actively discern. As we've seen, self-awareness in the light of God is searing, laser-accurate, and sometimes painful but always liberating, never vindictive. It inspires and encourages us to change where the harsh judgment we direct at ourselves leads only to spinning our wheels and at root is a form of self-hatred. A story about Abba Ephraim brings out some sense of what it is like to live under the gaze of God:

> Once when Abba Ephraim was passing by there was a whore who approached him at somebody's instigation, and she fawned on him to move him to shameful intercourse, or at least to anger, for nobody had ever seen him being angry or contentious. But he said to her, "Follow me." Approaching a place where there were very many people, he said to her, "Here in this place, do what you wanted to," but she, seeing the crowd, said to him, "How can we do it in the presence of such a crowd?" He said to her, "If you are ashamed before folk, how ought we not to be ashamed before God who reproved 'the hidden things of darkness'?" [see 1 Cor 4:5]. She went away ashamed.[14]

The abba is not prudish and does not run off scandalized at the woman's suggestions. In fact he is willing to play along. He lives transparent to the light of God and knows the passions that are within him; he is used to constantly exposing them to the light and warmth of divine love, for healing. He demonstrates the healthy shame that is an awareness of his limits, the shame that is the root of humility and "source of spirituality," where the woman is shown to be playing a part, not acting sincerely. Perhaps she exchanges an unhealthy shame, a sense of worthlessness clothed in the role of seductress, for a right sense of the crassness of her actions.[15]

Again, there is a difference between allowing our actual limits to come to light and attempting to seize control or shore up our esteem by imposing some outside standard. "Abba Isaiah said, 'Simplicity and not measuring oneself

[14] *The Book of the Elders*, 149.

[15] For healthy shame as the foundation of humility and "the source of spirituality": John Bradshaw, *Healing the Shame That Binds You* (Deerfield Beach, FL: Health Communications, 1988), vii.

purge [one] of wicked *logismoi* [thoughts].' "[16] Fighting passions with passions only reinforces passions. By simplicity we allow ourselves to be seen as we are, without pretense. If we impose a measure against which we evaluate ourselves, or in terms of which we present ourselves to others, we invite "wicked thoughts" and delusional narratives. Simplicity also carries the sense of the purity of heart that is "to will one thing." When our heart is set on the One who alone is good and not merely on the good that is no more than the opposite of evil and a matter of human convention, all the powers within us are energized and competing thoughts fall away.

In other words, the best way to purge our hearts of less worthy, distracting desires is to live fully from the deepest desire of our hearts. Not that distracting passions and "thoughts" cease to arise but they have nowhere to get a foothold. Knowing that distractions will always abound is itself an element of discernment. All kinds of unwanted thoughts and movements arise but while there is a powerful impulse to identify with what we are thinking and feeling, *we are not our thoughts*. So often the thought with which we identify is a judgment: I'm terrific, I'm detestable, I'm not as healthy, attractive, intelligent as this person or that. But any such measure means we have already stepped out of the flow of life and so whatever insight or resolve we arrive at will be lacking.

The same holds when we measure another. The self who judges and the self who is judged arise together and are both illusions, conceptual idols. In practice, when another person gets under our skin there's a strong tendency to effectively reduce that person to the trait or behavior that provokes in us such a strong response. In fact, they may

[16] *The Book of the Elders*, 149.

bear only a trace of this or that characteristic but because of our particular sensitivity, it appears magnified. The splinter becomes a beam. Even when reliable others corroborate our view our passions interfere. Discernment involves awareness that such "static" is in play and a determination to act toward the other person *as if* there is more to them than what annoys us.

Abba Macarius suggests one approach: "If we keep in remembrance the bad things said to us by people, we are suppressing the power of the remembrance of God; but if we keep the bad things in remembrance as though said to us by demons, we will be unharmed."[17] This can be a helpful strategy. We are all made in the image of God, and are his children; we are all on the same side, battling against the demons and the passions through which they attack us. The enemy loves nothing more than when we turn on one another. When we "demonize" others we reduce the mystery of their being to an abstraction. Macarius suggests a countermeasure: not idealizing, but *humanizing* them by locating the root of what is evil in the demons and not in a human nature that is made in the divine image.

If we keep in our hearts a contemplative "remembrance of God" it will in time dissolve or transform any resentment that may arise. If we deliberately foster and enflame resentment we lose sight of God and his goodness. We can't will both at once. The more we cultivate remembrance of God, of his goodness, and the great mercy he's shown us, the harder it becomes to judge others. The more we stew over the wrongs done to us, working ourselves up into a vengeful froth, the more we dam up the channel of grace. Again, it is not the feelings of anger or resentment that are the problem. These are largely out of our control and in themselves may

[17] *The Book of the Elders*, 154.

be accurate and even helpful emotions. Rather, it's the intentional kindling of wrath that's destructive. It's not the one who simply feels anger, but the one who says in his heart, "You fool," that is liable to judgment, just as a person is not condemned for sexual stirrings but the intentional "look" that reduces the other to a tool, an object of gratification.

Contemplative Prayer

We need to cultivate an interior space of not judging in order to see just how judgmental we are; to perceive and begin to heal the root of that self-righteousness. Contemplative prayer, "remembrance of God," is a deep interior form of not judging. In stillness and quiet, allowing whatever thoughts that arise to come into the light of God's presence, we practice not reacting but getting close, even to intensely afflictive thoughts and feelings. While discernment includes insight into our passions, how we've been shaped by our past, what triggers us and why, it is not reducible to insight alone but involves inhabiting the wound, feeling the pain and tension held in our bodies and listening to what it has to say. The "peace" the desert fathers speak of is not the pacification of difficult feelings by the imposition of technique but the grace of a peace that "surpasses understanding," a peace in the midst of stress and conflict.

When our hearts are deeply at rest we see other people in a different light. It's easier to intuit something of their dignity as icons of God, despite a sometimes disfigured surface. If we make it a top priority to cultivate and deepen the gift of interior peace we will be less prone to engage in the sort of judgment that stirs up turmoil. Not that we avoid conflicts that need to be faced but rather we find a way into them without getting highjacked by our passions. Again, not by suppressing those passions but precisely by attunement to them.

Merton wrote of contemplative prayer in these terms:

> Contemplative prayer is, in a way, simply the preference for the desert, for emptiness, for poverty. One has begun to know the meaning of contemplation when he intuitively and spontaneously seeks the dark and unknown path of aridity in preference to every other way. The contemplative is one who would rather not know than know. Rather not enjoy than enjoy. Rather not have *proof* that God loves him. He accepts the love of God on faith, in defiance of all apparent evidence. This is the necessary condition, and a very paradoxical condition, for the mystical experience of the reality of God's presence and of his love for us. Only when we are able to "let go" of everything within us, all desire to see, to know, to taste, and to experience the presence of God, do we truly become able to experience that presence with the overwhelming conviction and reality that revolutionize our entire inner life.[18]

In light of our discussion, we can see how an attitude of unknowing and an awareness of the fundamental emptiness of thoughts and feelings supports harmony, where the need to insist on being right, nailing down just what that means and convincing others, stirs discord. Grounding in the reality of divine love takes place at a level before thoughts and feelings, before even the sense of self such that whatever arises at the level of thoughts and feelings is seen at a distance, becomes transparent, and is less likely to become a point of contention. Why fight over thoughts and feelings that are fundamentally empty, over questions where more is unknown than known? Just as "The monk who truly

[18] Thomas Merton, *Contemplative Prayer* (New York: Herder and Herder, 1969), 111.

prays is unaware of prayer,"[19] the one who discerns in the Spirit has become transparent. Where the contentious self once used to be there's a bare space, and a preference for unknowing.

That divine love reaches us at our most vulnerable point. To come in from the cold and begin to thaw means to lose the protective shell of numb insensibility and feel the pain in our extremities as the blood starts to circulate. As we've seen, discernment involves awareness of and sensitivity to our weakness. Losing touch with our real condition, we develop a protective shell of judgments. In their fine work *Embracing Your Inner Critic: Turning Self-Criticism into a Creative Asset*, husband and wife team Hal and Sidra Stone write: "Whenever someone is not in touch with his or her vulnerability in relationship to another person, one may expect a judgment, silent or spoken, as a way of dealing with the situation."[20] They distinguish judgment from discernment by the sense of self-righteousness: "When we make judgments based on our disowned selves, we feel righteously correct. Out of this feeling of righteousness, we can justify almost any way of acting toward the other person. Noticing whether or not we feel righteous helps differentiate between judging and discerning. When we judge, we are righteous. When we are discerning, we are objective."[21] Learning to watch out for that feeling of self-righteousness, and to distrust it—to take a step back, recall our blind spots and fal-

[19] See John Cassian, *The Conferences*, trans. Boniface Ramsey (Mahwah, NJ: Newman Press, 1997): Cassian attributes to St. Antony the saying, "That is not a perfect prayer wherein the monk understands himself or what he is praying" (349).

[20] Hal and Sidra Stone, *Embracing Your Inner Critic: Turning Self-Criticism into a Creative Asset* (San Francisco: HarperSanFrancisco, 1993), 62.

[21] Stone, *Embracing Your Inner Critic*, 129.

libility, maybe consult an impartial third party—all good counsel.

Another element distinguishing discernment from judgment is the response of the other person. When we disown our own perfectionism, for instance, and condemn the same trait in someone else, the other person picks up a hardness or "edge" in our manner that makes them feel attacked: "Our judgments always have behind them a quality of righteousness. They convey an emotional impact, even when they are not spoken, and the person to whom they are directed always feels put down, no matter how subtle the judgment may be. Discernments are not righteous. They are much more impersonal and objective. There is no need to put the other person down in any way."[22]

We discern from a position "with and for" all others while we judge "over and against" some person or idea. Discernment is "both/and" where judgment is "either/or." Its views are held lightly and open to revision where judgment doubles down. Spiritual discernment is characterized by not knowing and making way where judgment needs to know prematurely, and to police the borders of what it considers to be right and wrong. In the mode of discernment we hold authority as a service used to support others in their uniqueness, whereas when we judge authority, it is seen as a privilege and imposed from without. The first is transparent while the second's opaque. Discernment is holistic rather than partisan and takes account of context and complexity where judgment has little room for either. It defers judgment to God where human judgment arrogates to itself the judgment that belongs to God alone. In an interview, Pope Francis identified this "both/and" approach as quintessentially Catholic:

[22] Stone, *Embracing Your Inner Critic*, 130.

Polarization is not Catholic. A Catholic cannot think either-or (*aut-aut*) and reduce everything to polarization. The essence of what is Catholic is both-and (*et-et*). The Catholic unites the good and the not-so-good. There is only one people of God. When there is polarization, a divisive mentality arises, which privileges some and leaves others behind. The Catholic always harmonizes differences. If we see how the Holy Spirit acts; it first causes disorder: Think of the morning of Pentecost, and the confusion and mess (*lío*) it created there, and then it brings about harmony. The Holy Spirit in the church does not reduce everything to just one value; rather, it harmonizes opposing differences. That is the Catholic spirit. The more harmony there is between the differences and the opposites the more Catholic it is. The more polarization there is, the more one loses the Catholic spirit and falls into a sectarian spirit. This [saying] is not mine, but I repeat it: what is Catholic is not either-or, but is both-and, combining differences. And this is how we understand the Catholic way of dealing with sin, which is not puritanical: saints and sinners, both together.[23]

[23] "Polarization Is Not Catholic," an interview with Pope Francis, *America* (January 2023): 19–20.

CHAPTER SEVEN

Hope

"If God is for us, who is against us?" (Rom 8:31). Who is it exactly God is for? "When you include everything, that is the real self" (Suzuki). So God is for the self that includes everything we are, the true person we are "in the image" of God, a reality that transcends every effort to construct and acquire an identity over against another. Instead of spurning God and becoming a law to oneself like those in Babel there's a Pentecostal harmonious cacophony, all sides and possibilities of myself brought to light, transformed and made to sing by the Spirit. "Who can be against us?" The one accused and the one who accuses are a co-fiction that arises together. The accuser reduces the other to the action for which they're accused, as though it defined them. Implicitly, they define themselves as one who is just, who has not committed such an action. Their own sins go into shadow along with the good actions (and intrinsic dignity) of the accused. When we are accused the temptation is to take the bait by substantiating, identifying with our role as accused, and the role of the other as accuser. We judge because we feel ourselves to be judged and we feel ourselves to be judged because we judge others. But God is for us. Through every disfiguration, he loves the latent image within us into realization.

We are so accustomed to think of "God" as a "judge" in our own image, one whose judgment is harsh and vengeful, that it's hard for us to grasp that in fact "God is for us." He is with and for us, a judge whose judgment is love, who judges only to liberate. As in his life on earth, Jesus reaches out to the man with the withered hand, the prostitute, the tax collector within us, shines a light on all we hold shameful—not to expose or humiliate but to heal and restore. From fear and shame and the resulting fierce attachment to "image management" we resist his efforts and obsessively try to photoshop away our real and imagined flaws. Often we co-opt religion into this project and dub this frantic scratching away of every blemish as "spiritual." We confuse God, who makes his rain and sun fall on just and unjust alike, with the merely human superego. God is for us, he wants us to flourish and be happy. He is for all of us, including the parts we turn away from. To the degree that we open these dark corners to his light we know the confidence and joy that comes from trust in his faithfulness.

As we will explore shortly, God is also for "all of us" in the sense of all persons. He supports and sustains the good of every human life, and desires that all come to salvation (see 1 Tim 2:4). God desires the good, the well-being of my enemy, which may include his being called to account. God is not on my side over against another. He is with and for the good of all. If we are to be perfect as our heavenly Father is perfect, we must also learn to be with and for all. Recall the words of Dostoevsky's Zosima: "Until one has indeed become the brother of all, there will be no brotherhood."[1] After the passage, "If God is for us, who is against us," Paul

[1] Fyodor Dostoevsky, *The Brothers Karamazov: A Novel in Four Parts with Epilogue*, trans. Richard Pevear and Larissa Volokhonsky (New York: Farrar, Straus and Giroux, 1990), 303.

writes: "He who did not withhold his own Son but gave him up for all of us, how will he not with him also give us everything else? Who will bring any charge against God's elect? It is God who justifies. Who is to condemn? It is Christ who died, or rather, who was raised, who is also at the right hand of God, who also intercedes for us" (Rom 8:32-34). As Bernard wrote, "In giving me himself, he gave me back myself." He restores us to our true nature so that we are "no longer slaves but sons," "no longer servants but friends [see John 15:15]."[2] Christ intercedes for us, he is our advocate, not our accuser. If his cross reveals our sins it is never to humiliate and punish, but always to liberate and heal.

In the parable of the two sons, it is when the prodigal has behaved least like a son that the father puts a ring on his finger and throws a banquet, that he most dramatically affirms, "You are my son." When the elder son delivers an even worse insult by refusing to greet guests on the father's behalf at the entrance to the banquet hall, the father humbles himself, goes out to plead with him and states, "Son . . . all that is mine is yours" (Luke 15:31). To accuse others is beneath our dignity as "sons." Allowing ourselves to be bullied by such self-appointed judges, too, is beneath our stature as children of God. In the words of another modern desert father, "Wanting to justify oneself is the act of a slave and not of a son of God."[3] As we saw with Bernard, the slave represents a state of mind dominated by fear, where we imagine God as a tyrannical master and act accordingly.

[2] Bernard of Clairvaux, *On Loving God*, with an analytical commentary by Emero Stiegman, CF 13B (Collegeville, MN: Cistercian Publications, 1995), 18.

[3] Silouane the Athonite, quoted in Mary Wolff-Salin, *No Other Light: Points of Convergence in Psychology and Spirituality* (New York: Crossroad, 1989), 204.

Fear prompts us to endlessly defend and justify ourselves against real and imagined accusations. At the opposite end of the spectrum, the summit of the spiritual life in the desert tradition is marked by the willingness to bear insult and accusation with meekness and patience precisely because we've come to know and "believe the love that God has for us" (1 John 4:16).

The Crucified

In his profound and highly original work *The Crucified Jesus Is No Stranger*, Sebastian Moore develops an account of self-hatred as the heart of "original sin" through his understanding of the crucified Christ as the image of the self. We ignore the deep, that is whole, self and the fullness of life it represents in favor of the needy ego.[4] Jesus embodies "this dreaded yet desired self," such that "the crucifixion of Jesus then becomes the central drama of a person's refusal of his or her true self." The cross reveals and makes explicit both how we destroy our true self and that even this is forgiven.[5] Indeed, he forgave even this so that we would not doubt that we are totally accepted.[6] The cross is seen as the dialogue between who God made us and who we have made ourselves.[7] It displays the full reality of our condition as at once crucifier and crucified. Encountering Christ involves the heart-rending discovery of the goodness and wholeness to which we were called and the brutal caricature we've become. As discussed earlier, we are thrown

[4] Sebastian Moore, *The Crucified Jesus Is No Stranger* (Mahwah, NJ: Paulist, 1977), xiv–xv.

[5] Moore, *The Crucified*, xv.

[6] Moore, *The Crucified*, 5.

[7] Moore, *The Crucified*, 89.

into the world helpless and long before we are free enough to deliberately sin, suffer at the hands of others. Tragically, we tend to internalize that violence and turn it against ourselves in an effort to control it, heaping abuse on our own original wholeness. In such a fashion we are crucified and further crucify ourselves.

Needless to say, this kind of monastic depth psychology is not the only lens through which to read the Christian mystery but it supplies an essential dimension and makes the person of Christ of intimate and burning concern to each of us in our interior journey, our desire for him inseparable from our inmost desire for our own realization so that, as Moore writes: "We cling to the figure on the cross not with the desperation of one in search of a savior but with the passion with which we embrace the being that God calls us to."[8] The validation and realization of our true self "in God" for Moore is what we are made for: "The greatest happiness possible, and the very definition of happiness, is to be oneself without inhibition."[9] "Self" here has the Jungian sense Moore describes as "the obscurely perceived totality of a person's life as a reality able to become conscious and to be a source of psychic energy far in excess of and more far-reaching than the self of which we are readily and inescapably conscious and that we call ego. My life is so much more than me."[10]

Moore views sin as a repudiation and hatred of our own wholeness manifest in Jesus. "One hates oneself free from sin." It is this self-hatred in which we relentlessly tear ourselves apart from which Christ frees us: "Jesus does not take us off the cross, but he frees us from putting ourselves

[8] Moore, *The Crucified*, 18.
[9] Moore, *The Crucified*, 22.
[10] Moore, *The Crucified*, 24.

there."[11] Moore sees that self-hatred is not simply a roadblock to divine love but the medium through which that love is communicated: "One's self-hatred is not only the *obstacle* to one's acceptance of God's love. It is the *medium* in which God's love is revealed to us as it transforms it . . . God does not just give me a *reason* not to hate myself. He transforms my self-hatred into love. That is the meaning of the cross."[12] As in the Japanese art of *kintsugi* ceramic repair, where the crack pattern in a shattered vessel is filled with gold and becomes the feature of a new design, the very shape of our innermost brokenness becomes the channel for a new creation.

In Moore's view, sin has the effect of fundamentally suppressing our own integrity and depriving others of the unique manifestation of the divine each of us was made to be. Squelching our brightest possibilities is the root way we betray God and hurt others.[13] For Moore, violence toward others cannot exhaust the hatred that is originally aimed at oneself: "Our self-hatred is not adequately expressed in the interactive process of violence provoking violence. It resides in the heart of the human that is the seat of evil. Our heart is not converted simply by seeing that the other to whom our violence is directed does not return it. Our heart is converted by seeing that one's violence is directed to oneself: to oneself dramatized in the symbol of Jesus crucified where he (man) appears as most lovable and most hated, and, in sorrow and pardon, most whole."[14] Earlier we touched on the figure of Mary at the foot of the cross. Her presence gains a new depth in light of Moore's reflection.

[11] Moore, *The Crucified*, 30.
[12] Moore, *The Crucified*, 47–48; italics original.
[13] Moore, *The Crucified*, 47–48.
[14] Moore, *The Crucified*, 32.

Just as Mary knew best of all the goodness God was giving the world in Jesus, and saw most clearly the cruelty and delusion of those who so brutally rejected him, so too she grieves and bears witness to the manner in which we reject and despise our freedom, our true nature as sons in the Son. She holds together anguish and profound serenity.

Universal Communion

As we've touched on, while often we must learn to accept something in ourselves before we can accept it in others, sometimes the struggle to accept something in another allows us to accept it in ourselves. Sometimes, perhaps most often, both processes are in play at once. While the desert fathers focus on their own inner work and relationships within their immediate community, how might their stress on not judging apply in the wider social world? How might it apply on the macro level of national or even international affairs?

The further we get from our immediate circle the more guarded and less generous we tend to become. The very scale of the conflicts works against sane and compassionate action. So much lies outside our influence. Of course it's necessary to start where we are. Suzuki advised: "We say, to shine one corner of the world—that is enough. Not the whole world. Just make it clear where you are." Any wider impact will flow from being fully present right where we are and embracing the limits and possibilities of our immediate context.

Gabriel Marcel wrote, "As readers of newspapers we can only despair . . . We have no way of getting a grip on the more or less truncated world that newspapers offer to our attention." After stating that the kinds of action that follow from reading the news (protests, petitions) are essentially "hopeless," he writes, "I am convinced that only in the quite limited sphere of activity that belongs to us and in which each of us bears responsibility, it is only within this sphere that hope can live."[15] He continues by suggesting that prayer acquires its real meaning in the arena of the everyday battle with despair, in ourselves and others. Describing despair as sin insofar as it resists "universal communion" and fixates on self, he writes: "There can be no sectarianism of hope; hope is emptied of its meaning and its virtue if it is not the affirmation of a we, of an all-of-us-together—but this oneness of spirit can of course be founded only upon an appeal to the One."[16] The way to this "universal communion" lies precisely through the embrace of our unique and particular contexts instead of seeking solace in the apparent clarity of fixed (ideological) positions.

In the context of interreligious dialogue, for instance, there are those, often not very deeply embedded in a particular tradition, who like to imagine a mystical level that floats above the messiness and naivete of traditional religious views and practice, which at best are seen to lead beyond themselves to this higher generic mystical state. Instead, it may be more helpful to imagine a common root, one vine launching out shoots wildly in all directions, one life with many expressions and no need for them to fall into neat patterns of visible symmetry and alignment. In politics, an analogous language of toothless generalities often provides cover for power plays by which nation-states suck up all power into themselves and away from smaller scale

[15] In every case? For my part I would want to qualify this and say that to the degree that "activism" is about contending abstractions divorced from the real lives of actual people in their concrete lives it is hopeless.

[16] Gabriel Marcel, "The Structure of Hope," *Communio* 23, no. 3 (Fall 1996): 611.

organizations closer to the ground. As we've seen, *The Brothers Karamazov* dramatizes this tendency by setting the Grand Inquisitor parable of Ivan alongside the depiction of the emerging paternalistic state which has begun to take over from the church responsibility for those in need.

Some of the dynamics of the inner life find a parallel in wider fields of relationship. If our true nature is like that of the father in the parable, both stable and generous, non-judging, while a reckless younger and indignant elder son chase each other in circles, something like that seems to happen outside as well with judge and accused trading places: one side overbearing and moralistic in matters of personal morality while the other is permissive and slack. Then the slack grow tight and start policing the less than civil language and views of their rival. Bracketing any adjudication of which position may be closer to the truth in a given case, it's possible to see these kinds of dynamic in play, distorting both positions, and weakening the chance for any meaningful exchange. Any kind of common ground becomes further and further away.

At the Second Vatican Council, John XXIII said famously that Catholics and Christians of other churches shared more than what divided them, a statement that implied (and demonstrated) a simple but profound shift in paradigm. Baptism and belief in the gospel held more weight than divisions which, while based on real enough disagreements, had grown infected by centuries of rivalry and discord. In *Fratelli Tutti* it seems to me Pope Francis has extended this view to include the entire human family: we share more than what divides us. In the common experience of shared human life there is a profound basis for cooperation and understanding. All of us are born into the world, experience loss, suffering, uncertainty. All of us face illness and death, know joy and sorrow.

While Vatican II spoke of Christians in other churches in greater or lesser degrees of "communion" with Rome, Francis has extended the language of "communion" to include the entire human family.[17] The global Covid pandemic that formed the context for *Fratelli Tutti* brought to light the extent of human interconnection (and division), and showed, as Francis writes, "no one is saved alone; we can only be saved together."[18] In a similar vein, in *Let Us Dream: The Path to a Better Future*, he states: "For a long time we carried on thinking we could be healthy in a world that was sick. But the crisis has brought home how important it is to work for a healthy world."[19]

Francis is keenly alert to the ways "a permanent state of disagreement and confrontation" can be generated and used as a means of political manipulation.[20] In the American context, for instance, a tiny portion of the population controls a vastly disproportionate amount of wealth and engenders discord between poor white and poor non-white communities to distract them from their common oppressor and forestall their cooperation. Francis laments the lack of "common horizons" and suggests even that World War III is underway and already being fought piecemeal (as though we were too divided to hold even a properly "world" war!).[21] He depicts a contemporary form of "judging" as the urge to airbrush away whatever runs contrary to our tastes and preferences: "A mechanism of selection then

[17] Pope Francis, Encyclical Letter *Fratelli Tutti* of the Holy Father Francis on Fraternity and Social Friendship 149 (October 3, 2020).

[18] Francis, *Fratelli Tutti* 32.

[19] Francis, *Let Us Dream: The Path to a Better Future; Pope Francis in Conversation with Austin Ivereigh* (New York: Simon and Schuster, 2020), 30.

[20] Francis, *Fratelli Tutti* 15.

[21] Francis, *Fratelli Tutti* 26.

comes into play, whereby I can immediately separate likes from dislikes, what I consider attractive from what I deem distasteful. In the same way, we can choose the people with whom we choose to share our world. Persons or situations we find unpleasant or disagreeable are simply deleted in today's virtual networks; a virtual circle is then created, isolating us from the real world in which we are living."[22]

Elsewhere in *Fratelli Tutti* he speaks of those who "define themselves in opposition to others," and, in *Let Us Dream*, describes "the selective morality of ideology."[23] For Francis, we ought instead to work toward an "integral ecology" and a "social friendship that excludes no one and a fraternity that is open to all," even the recognition that "every person is immensely holy."[24] Starkly, he warns that without the recognition of the intrinsic dignity and worth of each human person there is simply no future for humanity.[25]

Francis identifies "the isolated conscience" which prompts us to cut ourselves off from our community, "closing us in on our own interests and viewpoints by means of suspicion and supposition," which in turn makes us into "beleaguered, complaining selves who disdain others, believing that we alone know the truth."[26] Discussing this

[22] Francis, *Fratelli Tutti* 47.

[23] Francis, *Fratelli Tutti* 89; *Let Us Dream*, 35.

[24] Francis, *Let Us Dream*, 35; *Fratelli Tutti* 94, 195.

[25] Francis, *Fratelli Tutti* 107; perhaps there is at least a suggestion here that if we cannot be "saved" alone on earth we cannot be eternally saved in isolation.

[26] Francis, *Let Us Dream*, 69; a few pages later (76) Francis explicitly connects his argument with the desert tradition when he links the phrase "suspicion and supposition" to a text from Dorotheos of Gaza: "Don't let the wrong you think another has done to you trigger your descent into the isolated conscience. As Dorotheos puts it, 'Suspicions and suppositions are full of malice and never leave the soul in peace.' "

tendency in terms of church politics, he notes that both traditionalist and "revolutionary" wings can fall into the trap. He notes a certain rigidity and authoritarianism characteristic of those seeking to impose their particular slant on the church and finds that this rigidity is a source of concealment. When such rigidity is present, before long corruption, abuse of power, and other scandals come to light.[27]

Francis holds that the "antibody" to the "virus" of the isolated conscience is "self-accusation" in place of the accusation of others. This language could be misleading in a couple of respects. For one, it suggests that we are doing the same kind of thing only with ourselves as the target instead of another. In fact, as we've seen, when we judge another we are most often disowning some part of ourselves we fear or dislike. It's an escape from responsibility and a distortion of truth. By contrast, when we fully acknowledge our part in a conflict, we take responsibility in a realistic way that clarifies the situation. For another, we've seen how many—a victim of abuse, for instance—take too much of the wrong kind of "responsibility" by punishing themselves instead of holding the abuser accountable. This can operate in quite subtle ways with expert "gaslighters" manipulating their victims into questioning themselves and excusing the guilty.[28]

In Francis's view polarization, while exacerbated by "some media and some politicians," has a "spiritual root" in the devil as "the Great Accuser." He warns against engaging with the enemy on its own terms, reacting in kind,

[27] Francis, *Let Us Dream*, 70.

[28] In a way "accusation" here holds the same kind of equivocal meaning we've seen throughout with "judgment" and "anger"—the same word is doing too much work and covering irreconcilable things.

arguing with the devil: "Instead of letting ourselves become trapped within the labyrinth of accusation and counter-accusation, which conceals the bad spirit in a tissue of false reasons and justifications, we need to allow the bad spirit to reveal itself. This is what Jesus teaches us from the Cross. In gentleness and powerlessness, he forced the devil to show himself: the Accuser confuses silence with weakness, and redoubles his attack, revealing his fury, and thereby who he is."[29]

In no way is the "power made perfect in weakness"—Jesus forgiving his enemies from the cross, walking the extra mile, turning the other cheek—a floating above the fray or evasion of conflict. It is precisely peace in the heart of trial and discord. Francis is working out here what this attitude can look like applied in the widest fields of politics and culture. The temptation is either to reduce opposing views to absolute contraries or to downplay and evade real conflict. The approach Francis maps out, a contemporary, macro scale ethos akin to the spirit of not judging in the desert tradition, involves remaining in polarized spaces, "holding" disagreement in a way that keeps the tension and

[29] Francis, *Let Us Dream*, 77. A recent article hits the nail on the head: "The fundamental problem with politics is that it is conducted entirely in the voice of The Accuser. Whereas Jesus repeatedly warns us in the strongest possible terms not to judge others, politics, especially American party politics, draws most of its power from judgmentalism. It attributes all blame to the other tribe and none to its own; it is constantly on the attack, isolating and amplifying the other tribe's flaws; and it reduces people to caricatures of their opinions, seeing no goodness in them personally or in their motives. That technique is ubiquitous, regardless of where one falls on the political spectrum. And it is poisonous." Julia Hejduk, "A Medicinal Warning for My Pro-Life Friends," *Church Life Journal*, January 13, 2023, https://churchlifejournal.nd.edu/articles/some-side-effects-of-politics-a-medical-warning-for-my-pro-life-friends/.

stays open to it becoming creative, to "new thinking," a new direction emerging from apparently intractable positions.

The Impossible Story

On the personal level, we experience the mercy of God and take a tentative step on the path of not judging, exhilarated by a new sense of peace and freedom . . . then out of fear fall back into the compulsive need to create a sense of self by opposition. We lurch between the sense of abundance and possibility opened by the experience of grace and the constricted punitive storylines woven by sin. In his study of Julian of Norwich, Denys Turner insightfully brings out the way the two horizons awkwardly coexist. While, as he writes, the view of the prodigal son held by the father, and that of the elder son, cannot both be true, "yet both have real force and agency in the world that human beings inhabit. Or to put it in another way, more often than not we attempt to live within and think through our lives' meaning in terms of both stories together . . . Because of sin we are fractured selves. So to speak, in our substance we inhabit the story that love tells and in our sensualite we inhabit the story that sin tells—or, more precisely, in our fallen condition we inhabit the impossible story that is neither because it attempts to tell both stories at once."[30]

If this ambivalence marks the personal level it's not hard to see how much more pervasive it becomes at the social. It accounts for the split in Christian imagination and tradition between the reality and power of grace and the fear of a vengeful deity. Every time Christians bracket the demands of the gospel for the sake of *realpolitik*, the elder son prevails

[30] Denys Turner, *Julian of Norwich, Theologian* (New Haven, CT: Yale University Press, 2011), 206.

and the way of the father is brushed aside as extravagant and irresponsible.

The story of guilt and suffering told by love and that told by sin aligns with our account of "judgment" as opposed to spiritual discernment: the "us versus them" view dominated by a spirit of faction and rivalry, and the way of the gospel: a love that is with and for all. Turner underlines that coming to inhabit the horizon of grace is not the adoption of an intellectual point of view, the result of argumentation, but rather the fruit of an ongoing moral and spiritual transformation. As he describes, we experience a confused mixture of these two horizons, inspired by grace and constrained by fear. It's essential therefore to fully assimilate and be grateful for the touches of grace we've experienced. The liturgy, especially the Eucharist, along with personal engagement with scripture allow the seeds that such touches of grace implant to root down and begin to grow.

Hopefully our reflection on the *Sayings* of the desert fathers has helped to clarify what these two ways of experiencing the world are like, so that we can recognize the reactivity and constriction of fear and the expansiveness and freedom of grace when they arise in our hearts, and find courage to "be guided by the Spirit" (Gal 5:25). It's not a matter of willpower. "*Awareness* is the greatest agent for change."[31] As our brokenness becomes transparent, we begin to leave room for grace to open up situations that seemed to be hopelessly stuck. We cooperate with God in turning all things to good (see Rom 8:28). A short reflection on the Japanese art of ceramic repair (*kintsugi*) provides a sense of what that can look like.[32]

[31] Eckhart Tolle, *A New Earth: Awakening to Your Life's Purpose* (New York: Penguin Books, 2016), 99.

[32] For examples of kintsugi, see https://www.adsoftheworld.com/campaigns/kintsugi-pieces-in-harmony-turkey-armenia.

"Mend to Make New"

Proposing "culture care" as an alternative to the pervasive "culture war" mentality, artist and peacemaker Makoto Fujimura writes of "mending to make new" instead of seeking to "fix" a broken object or relationship.[33] He uses the Japanese art of kintsugi ceramic repair to illustrate. Kintsugi involves the careful, meditative refitting of the broken fragments of a cherished vessel in which the cracks are accentuated rather than erased, filled in with gold, with the pattern of fracture lines forming a new design, the repaired bowl, cup, or plate valued even more highly than the original.

The creative transformation of chance cracks into the basis of a new design is highly suggestive and has struck a chord in popular culture, the basic corollary being the way our wounds and weak points can become our greatest strengths. Fujimura develops the Christian symbolism of kintsugi, stressing how the risen Christ appeared, not with his wounds erased but with light streaming through those very "holy and glorious wounds," wounds which become the signs of his authenticity. It is said that the devil can appear in a likeness of Christ but can never appear with the wounds. These are the jealously guarded trophy of the true Christ alone. By the presence or absence of the wounds, visionaries can distinguish between Christ and a deceptive imitation.

Fujimura contrasts the contemporary western ethos/aesthetic of mass industrialized culture where the irregular is a defect and the broken is thrown away or at best "fixed" to the spirit of kintsugi: "First, we need a realignment of

[33] See Makoto Fujimura, chap. 4, "Kintsugi Theology," in *Art and Faith: A Theology of Making* (New Haven, CT: Yale University Press, 2020), 41–60; and Makoto Fujimura and Susannah Black Roberts, "Making Art to Mend Culture," *Plough* (Winter 2023).

our understanding of beauty beyond a Western, industrialized, cosmetic, concept toward that of a maculate, broken beauty of the East. The divide in ideology, both on the conservative and liberal side, has roots in the binary 'scapegoating' of what we see as unforgivable imperfections. We see such fractures only through the immaculate lens that our ideological idols demand."

Fujimura enjoins taking up our own brokenness not to blame and suppress, but with a view to its creative transformation, finding in its very lineaments the design of a new work: "Art can bring somatic, reflective, deeper contemplation that moves us away from blaming others (or any politicians) to asking instead, 'What is in me to mend, to make new?' When we do that, when we behold deeply of our own souls and the edges of our fractures, we will find that we need each other and communities (even our enemies) to find complete healing."[34] As suggested here, the first step in kintsugi repair is the mindful admiration of the fragments, in their brokenness, without any thought of "fixing" them, gluing them back together as if they'd never been damaged. There's a verse in the *Tao Te Ching*, "If you want to be whole, be partial," which I take to mean, wholeness comes through fully inhabiting our brokenness.

But what happens when a vessel is broken beyond any possibility of elegant repair, when some of the fragments are no more than dust? Here a form of kintsugi called *yobitsugi*[35] comes into play, in which shards from one bowl or cup are grafted onto another to form a patchwork quilt or pottery collage to very striking effect. Fujimura describes the work of one contemporary yobitsugi artist, Rokujigen,

[34] Fujimura and Roberts, "Making Art," 59.

[35] For a modern example of *yobitsugi*, see https://www.thepoiroom.co.nz/products/yobitsugi-large-vase.

who has fashioned together halves of (different) ceramic plates, one each from countries at war, with the line of gold joining them following the contours of the contested border between them (India/Pakistan, divided Ireland, and so on). To conclude this reflection on not judging, I'd like to suggest how this yobitsugi ethical aesthetic might work out across several levels.

In terms of our awareness, what if we were simply to allow the scattered, disjointed shards—insights, sensations, ad jingles, random memories, compulsions—to rest alongside one another just as they are, with no thought of "fixing" our mind to conform with some preset expectation of how it should be? Simply to notice such ephemera with care and attention changes our relation to it. With a troubling sensation or memory, or even with an insight or inspiration, simply remaining with the "shard" in stillness opens the door to a way of "mending to make new."

A watchword throughout this book has been the saying of Shunryu Suzuki, "When you include everything, that is the real self." What if we imagine the self as a yobitsugi bowl, a patchwork of jarring, even discordant elements carefully arranged and bound together into an elegant whole? No one part set against the rest can claim to be the complete vessel yet somehow the emptiness of the bowl holds it all together. So, by humility, the father of the two sons becomes a clearing, a place of not judging where his rival sons can meet, where both sons are honored as sons when they least act like it. The disfigured shards are cherished.

In our immediate communities—family, friends, workplace, parish—we can slow our response to discord and seek to find grounds for new combinations in the midst of apparent disharmony. Fujimura writes: "As the broken body of Christ, the church must lead in the way of modeling such mending to the fractured, suffering world. We are to value people and their differences, each with a unique journey of brokenness. We must remember that we as Christians are a mosaic of broken pieces, only coming together in Christ. Art dedicated to kintsugi generation can be the bridge to invite skeptical folks into an authentic community of brokenness, only made beautiful by our kintsugi Savior."[36]

In the wider field of politics and culture too, we can see how the yobitsugi ethos might apply, as we navigate the twofold temptation Pope Francis describes: on the one hand to reduce positions in (potentially creative) tension to airtight ideological contraries, and on the other to elude conflict altogether in a vain hope to float above the fray. Neither a passive escape from tension nor a matter of constraint and striving, "not judging" appears as a liberating, deeply contemplative way to allow intractable conflict to yield to surprising and creative new configurations.

[36] Fujimura and Roberts, "Making Art," 59.